Genghis Khan

An Enthralling Guide to the Conquests, Empire, and Enduring Legacy of the Mongol Horde

Free limited time bonus

We forget 90% of everything
that we've read in 7 days...

Get the free printable pdf summary of
the book you've read AND much, much
more... shhhh...

Enter Your Most Frequently Used Email to Get Started

**DOWNLOAD FREE PDF
SUMMARY**

© Enthralling History

Stop for a moment. We have a free bonus set up for you. The problem is this: we forget 90% of everything that we read after 7 days. Crazy fact, right? Here's the solution: we've created a printable, 1-page pdf summary for this book that you're reading now. All you have to do to get your free pdf summary is to go to the following website: **https://livetolearn.lpages.co/enthrallinghistory/**

Or, Scan the QR code!

Once you do, it will be intuitive. Enjoy, and thank you!

Table of Contents

Introduction: From Small to Great

Genghis Khan. In many ways, the name seems to speak for itself. Just hearing it brings forth an image of great and unbridled conquest. The name is actually a title that means "Universal Ruler." Genghis Khan set himself up to be a universal ruler of his sprawling domain, which would ultimately stretch from China to Russia and beyond. It was a name that this historical figure earned, not one that he was born with.

As great as Genghis Khan one day became, he was actually born a relatively unknown nobody. Considering as much, some historians have drawn some rather startling historical analogies in regard to the fact that Genghis Khan was able to stunningly rise up onto the world stage from virtually out of nowhere. One historian stated that if Genghis Khan's rise had occurred back in the 1800s in the United States, it would have been akin to someone being born into slavery, only to rise up and forge a powerful movement—a movement that would engulf not just the United States but also all of North America and a huge chunk of South America. Yes, our hypothetical American Genghis Khan would have forged a mighty American empire.[i]

Born in late May 1162, Genghis Khan's name at birth was Temujin. He was born in the frigid wastes of Mongolia, a steppe country in central Asia. At the time of Temujin's arrival, the world was already a place of much tension and animosity. This was, after all, the time of the Crusades, in which much of the Middle East, North Africa, and the Near East were locked in religious power struggles.

---

[i] Nardo, Don. *Genghis Khan and the Mongol Empire.* 2010. Pg. 11.

The Mongols, however, were in a different world. In their backyard of the Eurasian Steppe, their main, immediate concern was establishing and maintaining dominance among the different tribes. Religion, for the most part, took a back seat to everyday survival. Sure, the Mongols enjoyed conversing with their wise shamans and soothsayers from time to time. And it is true that they occasionally sought to glean some information from the spirit world by way of fortune tellers. For instance, it has been said that after the future khan, Temujin, was born, his parents were beset by such wisemen. These wise and revered figures let it be known that young Temujin was destined to be a mighty warrior since he was born with a clot of blood clasped within his hand.[i]

Temujin's parents likely nodded their heads right along with the soothsayers' words, as if to say, "Well, that's nice." However, they knew that such pronouncements from soothsayers did not necessarily make or break Mongol society. Other than serving as a tool for personal guidance, it simply was not a part of the Mongol agenda to force religion—theirs or anyone else's—down anyone's throat.

The Mongolia of Genghis Khan's youth was full of constant tribal warfare. Truth be told, much of this warfare was actually engineered by outside forces, namely China. The Chinese had long feared the nomadic tribes to their north and had considered it prudent to make sure that the tribes fought each other instead of unifying and fighting China.

Yes, a long line of Chinese administrations employed the classic "divide and conquer" strategy. It is all rather Machiavellian, but you can hardly blame the Chinese for looking out for their own interests. The Chinese certainly were not the first world power to do such a thing, and they certainly were not the last. The Romans did it when they played various barbarian tribes lurking outside the borders of the Roman Empire against each other. They did not really like any of the tribes, but they also did not want any of them to get too powerful either. So, when one of the tribes started to get a bit too big for its britches, the Romans quietly backed the offending tribe's enemies in order to cut the upstarts back down to size.

The only trouble with constantly playing your less powerful neighbors against each other is that one day, they just might wise up to it. And despite one's best efforts to sow discord and confusion, they just might someday present a united front, perhaps even out of sheer spite.

[i] Humphrey, Judy. *Genghis Khan: World Leaders Past & Present.* 1987. Pg. 24.

Chapter 1: Early Life and Hardships

"He gave himself without restraint and with earnest zeal to every endeavor he undertook. He loved life for its own sake and did not trouble himself with searching for its meaning. He enjoyed it abundantly—with tranquil gaiety. Without perverse refinements—without inordinate passions. Jealous of his welfare and of his rights, but liberal, lavish towards others. He was keenly sensible of his glory and his grandeur, but without haughtiness and without vanity."

-Fernand Grenard

The future great ruler known as Genghis Khan was born with the name Temujin, a name that translates as "one who forges." There is some debate over the exact origin and meaning behind this name. Some have theorized that it was perhaps an aspirational name. Since it was likely common in those days for parents to name their children after professions (such as "Smith" with the aspiration of a child becoming a blacksmith forging metal), it is plausible that his name was a profession that his parents wished for him to one day have.

There is another altogether different theory about the origin of Temujin's name, though. As author and historian James Chambers has pointed out, it has been theorized that Temujin was actually the name of one of his father's defeated opponents who had taken him prisoner just before his own son—baby Temujin—was born.[ii]

[i] Hoang, Michel. *Genghis Khan*. 1988. Pg. 287.
[ii] Chambers, James. *Genghis Khan*. 2009. Pg. 26.

At any rate, the name would take on a far greater meaning when its bearer eventually went on to forge a mighty empire. Temujin—one who forges—was, therefore, a very fitting name.

The Onon River in Mongolia, which was near where Genghis Khan was born. [1]

Shortly after Temujin was born, his mother gave birth to another son named Kasar or Qasar. Kasar would come to stand by his brother's side during many of his later adventures, battles, and conquests. Kasar was followed by two more brothers—Khajiun and Temuge. The youngest child to be born was a daughter by the name of Temulun. He also had two half-brothers named Belgutei and Behter. These half-brothers were born to his father's other wives.

Yesugei had a growing family on his hands, and he likely worried about their future, as well as the future of the Mongolian steppes as a whole. It is believed that Temujin's father had tried and failed to fashion his own tribal confederation. He was a tribal leader, but that was only on a local level. He failed to reach his ultimate ambition of being a universal khan, but at the same time, he had come much closer to that goal than many of his warring predecessors had in the past.

Nevertheless, Yesugei was a man who was ready to look toward the future, and he was already considering the future for his young son Temujin. When Temujin was still just a small boy, Yesugei decided that he would find the child a prospective bride. Arranged marriages were a common custom among the Mongols, and selections were often made at a young age. These were essentially down payments on a matrimonial future, which would not be collected until many years later.

Yesugei took his young son Temujin on a trip toward the southeastern steppes near the border with China, where he intended to find a future bride for his son, handpicked from his mother Hoelun's own tribe. Apparently, any bad blood in regard to how Yesugei had bride-napped Hoelun from her own prospective husband did not seem to surface during this particular trip.

Yesugei came across a rich chieftain known as Dai Sechen, who was friendly enough and took an immediate liking to Temujin. Yesugei and Dai Sechen spoke with each other, and it was soon arranged for Temujin to become engaged to his daughter Borte. According to custom, this meant that Temujin would live with his prospective in-laws until his wedding day so that they would all get to know each other and become close.

As hard and awkward as it is for most of us in the modern world to get along with our in-laws, perhaps the Mongols were on to something! Being practically raised by one's in-laws likely created an exceptionally strong bond. One's in-laws would essentially be an additional set of adopted parents. As fate would have it, Temujin could use a set of spare parents, for his own father would not survive the trip back to his own tribe.

Although accounts seem to differ (as is often the case when it comes to the backstory of Genghis Khan), it is said that Temujin's father was somehow poisoned. According to one version of how this might have transpired, Yesugei was riding his horse when he came upon a group of herders who were traveling through the region. It was Mongolian custom to show hospitality to such travelers, so Yesugei stopped, chatted, and ate a meal with them.[i] Little did Yesugei know, but these travelers hailed from the Tatars—a tribal group that Yesugei had previously fought.

As an interesting aside, the Tatars have long been known as the Tartars. The addition of the "r" in the name has been attributed to Greek Orthodox Christians who cleverly nicknamed them that. Why? Well, these Eastern Christians who encountered the Tatars thought they were such hellions that they insinuated they were from Tartarus, the pits of hell.

The term Tartarus is only used once in the New Testament, and it is in reference to a hellish domain in which the fallen angels are said to be imprisoned. The Apostle Peter made the reference and purposefully used not just a Greek word but a Greek place name that pre-dated Christianity. In Greek mythology, Tartarus was where the Titans were

[i] Chambers, James. *Genghis Khan*. 2009. Pg. 29.

imprisoned. The Apostle Peter seems to be merging concepts together here. Or, then again, perhaps he is suggesting that the Titans and the fallen angels of the Bible are one and the same.

As it pertained to Yesugei and his encounter with these would-be denizens of Tartarus, the situation was initially friendly enough. In fact, the group apparently staged an impromptu dinner party and gave Yesugei plenty of alcohol to drink.

There was one problem, though—the alcohol had been laced with poison. It is unclear if Yesugei noticed anything being off about the flavor of his beverages that evening, but whatever he drank would certainly come back to get him later on.

Yesugei managed to make it back to his camp, but he knew that he was not going to live much longer. He summoned his friend and long-time servant Munlik (also spelled as Munglig) to his side and informed him of his dire situation. He also made a last-minute request.

He requested that Munlik head out to the camp where Temujin had been staying with his in-laws and have Temujin brought back at once. This was for the sheer practical reason that Temujin would be the man of the house with Yesugei's passing; he would be needed to help his widowed mother, Hoelun, get along.

Munlik was eager to oblige, but he knew that extracting a son from his in-laws was not an easy task. As such, he was sure to be as discreet about it as possible. Upon his arrival, he met the tribal chieftain and decided not to mention Yesugei's condition. He knew that if the chieftain realized that Yesugei was going to perish soon, he would have likely insisted on keeping his future son-in-law with him.

Instead, Munlik simply stated that Temujin's father missed his son and wished to see him one more time. Such a thing was a bit unusual, but considering the closeness of Yesugei and Temujin, the chieftain decided it would not hurt to oblige. He allowed Temujin to head off with Munlik for his "visit." However, that visit turned into a sad and bitter stay, as Temujin arrived to find his father dead. The burden of caring for his surviving family members was suddenly thrust on his young shoulders.

Yes, Temujin, who was only around ten years old, had to learn to grow up fast. He was considered a man of the house, so he needed to help take care of his recently widowed mother. Not a whole lot is known about Temujin's youth prior to his father's demise, but it was clearly his father's death that sent him on the trajectory of ultimately becoming a world-renowned figure in history.

Temujin apparently cared deeply for his mother, but it was a troubled relationship from the very start. Firstly, his mother, Hoelun, had been forced to be his father's bride. The Mongolians of this period had a long-standing tradition of kidnapping the brides of rivals. On Hoelun's wedding night to another man, Yesugei crashed the party. He threw her on the back of his horse and rode off. We can only imagine the tears that must have fallen as Hoelun realized that all of the dreams that she had envisioned with her previous fiancé had been viciously ripped away from her.

It is said that Yesugei held Hoelun hostage until she agreed to marry him. In this instance, the word "agree," of course, is a troubling one. Because what choice did she possibly have? With no hope of rescue and certainly no hope of any government denouncing her captor for war crimes, she ultimately acquiesced. She finally gave in and "agreed" to marry her kidnapper. Temujin—better known as Genghis Khan—was produced from this troubled union.

Even though the life that she lived was forced upon her, Hoelun had the small consolation that her new husband was a prominent tribal leader. This gave her a sense of encouragement since her son was the heir apparent of a small but growing tribal confederation.

However, after Yesugei died, all bets were off. The locals did not respect Hoelun once her husband was dead. They viewed her and her children by him as more or less a nuisance to be spurned. This was a sad

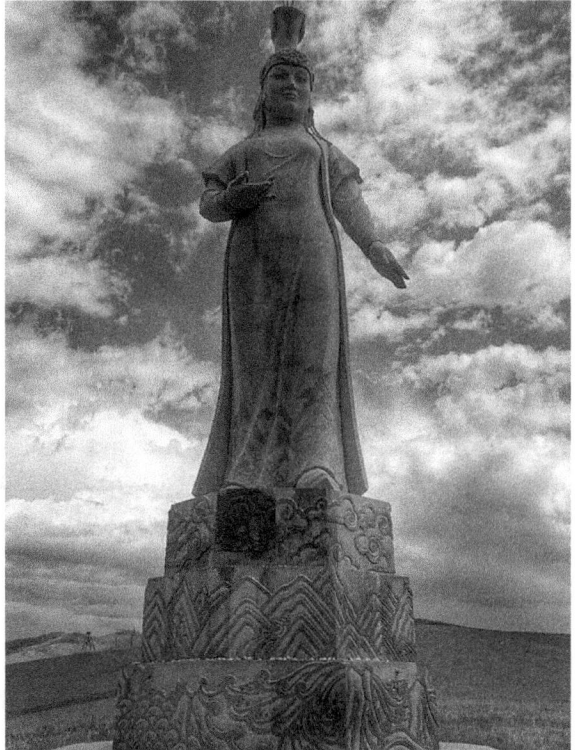

A statue of Hoelun. [2]

and bitter fate for a woman who had been kidnapped, then forced to become a bride and mother, only to be widowed and disrespected by the kinsmen of her deceased kidnapper-turned-husband. But this was indeed what life seemed to have in store for poor Hoelun.

The first summer after Yesugei's passing was the hardest since she and her family were virtually abandoned by the tribe. It was a wonder that the whole family did not perish during this lean period. It seems the only way they managed to eke out any sustenance to maintain their own existence was by the roots and berries that Hoelun gathered and the small game that Temujin and his brothers managed to catch.[i]

It was a hard life, and with such meager resources, tempers often flared. An argument over food allegedly led Temujin to get into an explosive argument with one of his brothers. He and Kasar had just caught a fish and were ready to bring it home for dinner when two of his brothers from one of his father's other wives—Bektor and Belgutei—came along, snatched up the fish, and took off with it.

Under more plentiful conditions, such an act could have been passed off as a mere childish prank. However, since the whole family was often just one fish or rabbit away from starvation, this was considered a serious offense. Temujin and his brother could not help but want to somehow get back at their brothers for what they had done. Soon, they found the perfect opportunity to do so.

The two brothers were out with their bows and arrows, ostensibly looking for more small game to fell and take home with them. But rather than coming across squirrels and rabbits, they came up right behind none other than their brother Bektor, who was apparently right in the midst of chowing down on the fish the two had just so painstakingly caught and which Bektor had so cruelly stolen.

Without saying a word, both Temujin and Kasar pulled back the arrows in their bows and fired upon their sibling. To this day, it is not clear which brother fired the fatal shot, but one of those arrows indeed found their mark, and Bektor was killed. This was done in the middle of a dark rage, and the boys seemed to immediately regret their actions. When they returned to Hoelun's tent, she seemed to be able to read the testimony of their dark act all over their faces.

---

[i] Humphrey, Judy. *Genghis Khan: World Leaders Past & Present.* 1987. Pg. 31.

She quickly got to the bottom of what had happened in a way that only a mother could, and upon learning the truth, she thoroughly denounced both of them. In her fury, she went as far as to call Temujin and Kasar savage beasts. Nevertheless, Hoelun knew there was no alternative but to try to forgive her sons so that they could do the best they could to move on with their lives.

Hoelun, in the meantime, was ready to take matters into her own hands. Fed up and tired of suffering from the cruel winds of fate, Hoelun decided to summon her own inner strength and do what she could to convince some of the tribal members to rally behind Temujin as the standard bearer of the tribe. However, the ten-year-old boy was a bit too young for most to consider rendering their allegiance to, but Hoelun's persistence eventually paid off. She managed to persuade a small fraction of the confederation to give Temujin a chance.

This shifting of a few dedicated souls was likely a blessing in disguise. It served to weed out those who were less serious and less loyal. This small faction that remained loyal to Temujin and his family would become the strongest and most able of allies in good time. Temujin would need them because there were plenty of rivals who would attempt to take advantage of his diminished confederation and try to snuff this would-be khan out before he had the chance to fulfill his destiny.

One of those who immediately rose up to challenge Temujin was a rival chief by the name of Targutai. It was Targutai who first decided to test the mettle of the new leader and launch a surprise attack against Temujin and his allies. Needless to say, they were not ready for it. Targutai and his forces charged right into Temujin's camp and were able to kill and loot almost at will. In the ensuing melee, young Temujin himself was forced to flee for his own protection.

Adding to his embarrassment, in the chaos, his mother was left behind. Targutai eventually made his way to Temujin's yurt, where Hoelun was holed up. Targutai was surprisingly respectful to Hoelun. He assured her that he did not wish her harm. He insisted that his fight was only with her son Temujin.

Targutai was indeed on the hunt for the young tribal leader and was soon sending his forces out to scour the surrounding steppe country to find him. Targutai knew that he could not have gotten far and that it would be just a matter of time before they would lay hold of him. He was right. Temujin and his followers were suffering while hiding in the brush and even inside caves. They desperately needed food. When Temujin was forced to leave one of their hiding spots to find something for his famished comrades to eat, he was spotted.

Targutai's men laid hold of the young khan, and to show how serious they were, they slapped a cangue around his neck. The cangue was a form of both punishment and restraint that was common in the region at the time. It consisted of a wooden brace that could be closed down over the head and shoulders of a prisoner, causing them to lose the mobility of their hands. Those locked inside the cangue had their hands stuck so far apart from their head that they were not able to use them for much of anything. Unless they were particularly gifted at throwing a piece of small fruit into their mouth, it was unlikely they could successfully feed themselves or even get a drink of water without assistance.

As such, while Temujin was in this state, he had a man who was put in place to guard him and occasionally feed and water him. He was completely dependent on the whims of his guard.

While Temujin was under the watch of this guard, Targutai and his warriors took off to have a celebratory feast. Targutai did not realize just how determined his young prisoner of war was. After the main group left and Temujin was alone with his sole guard, Temujin decided to act. He got behind his captor, and with all the strength he could muster, he slammed the corner of the wooden cangue that had him bound into the man's head. This sent the hapless guard to the ground, either in great pain or completely unconscious.

Temujin did not waste any time trying to find out. He fled from his oppressors and quickly disappeared into the surrounding wilderness. He had escaped. However, there was still one very big problem. The cangue, which had him bound, was still firmly locked around his neck. Hopefully, he at least got to get one last good drink of water and a morsel of food from his captor before he bonked him over the head since it was most certainly a long, harrowing trek across the steppe country.

Temujin was running on sheer adrenaline and reserves of strength, but he knew such things likely would not last for long. He had to find a solution to his dilemma, and he had to find one soon.

During his flight, he had a few fairly close calls. At one point, he heard members of Targutai's tribe riding behind him. He managed to drop down into a nearby river, as it was his only place to hide. Lying flat on his back, he submerged himself until only his mouth was just above the surface so that he could still breathe. His heart beat out of his chest as the group passed, but it seemed that no one saw him. But then, suddenly, one of the warriors did see him.

This warrior apparently looked Temujin right in the eye before suddenly looking away and curiously riding on. Who was this man? Why did he not alert his comrades as to what he had seen? Could he have been someone who secretly harbored pity for Temujin and his tribe?

It would later be learned that the man's name was Sorqan Shira and that he hailed from a group of steppe people referred to as the Suldus.[i] As it turns out, Sorqan had been forced to become a servant of Targutai's tribe, which helps to explain his indifference. He certainly did not have an interest in going out of his way to help those who were actively oppressing him.

As it were, Sorqan Shira did not say a word, and Targutai's warriors passed right on by. Temujin did not forget the kind stranger, and since he had no other option, he decided to follow the group. It has been said that he carefully watched from a distance as the group made their camp. Temujin took note of the man's yurt.

A yurt is a temporary dwelling that the Mongolians used. It is a circular structure similar to a teepee or tent in which warm material, such as animal skins, is wrapped around a wooden frame in order to create shelter. Temujin saw that the man entered and exited his yurt all by himself. He realized he was alone. Temujin then picked the perfect moment to sneak up to Sorqan's yurt. Since yurts typically don't have locked doors, he easily made his way inside.

The man was startled to see Temujin enter his yurt, and they were both likely very lucky that Sorqan did not shout out in sheer fright. Temujin, in his condition, certainly would have been a frightful sight. Dripping with water, the small, haggard face framed by the wooden cangue would have been downright spooky looking. The man almost thought he was looking at a ghost. But fortunately enough, he quickly calmed down, and Temujin was able to better explain his plight.

---

[i] Izzo, Robert. *The Life and Legend of Genghis Khan: Conquests, Power, Death, and the Mongol Empire.* 2020. Pg. 34.

Sorqan Shira agreed to help Temujin even further. It is said that he was able to bust the cangue right open before burning it to a crisp in an open fire. He did this to eliminate any sign of what had happened. Temujin was now, for all intents and purposes, free. But until he was able to distance himself from Targutai's camp, he was still in mortal danger.

Thankfully, the helpful stranger was able to aid him with this dilemma as well. He placed Temujin at the bottom of an oxcart and put wool on top of him. It was a crude hiding place, but it would serve its purpose until things had cooled down enough for Temujin to make his exit.

It was a good thing that the man hid Temujin like this because Targutai, desperate to find the escaped prisoner, had resorted to searching everyone's yurt in the encampment. Some of his agents soon came to the helpful stranger's yurt and looked around.

They saw the oxcart of wool, and it apparently occurred to them that someone might be hiding in it. All they had to do was brush the wool away with their hands, and they would have found Temujin. But these warriors chose a different approach. They took a spear and stabbed it into the cart. The accounts of what happens next seem to differ. Some say that the spear struck Temujin, but he was able to summon enough inner strength not to cry out in pain. Others, however, suggest that the spear luckily did not hit him.

The latter variation of this event seems more likely since it would be quite difficult not to make a sound when the razor-sharp tip of a spear is impaled into one's leg. But whatever the case may be, the warriors were apparently satisfied that nothing was in the cart and that no one else was in the yurt. They departed shortly thereafter.

Young Temujin was then able to get out of the cart and walk (or stumble, depending on the nature of his injuries) on his own two feet. His helpful new friend, Sorqan, was kind enough to gift him with a horse.

If this account is true, the future Mongol Empire would be built upon the kindness of this stranger. Without it, there would have been no Genghis Khan, and without Genghis Khan, there would have been no Mongol Empire.

Temujin jumped upon the beast and immediately rode back to his home encampment, where his mother Hoelun and his other kinsmen were already waiting for him.

Temujin had already survived many hardships by this point in his life. Indeed, life for him so far had been hard, but despite it all, he was determined to succeed.

Chapter 2: Solidifying His Hold

"These men, that is to say the Tartars, are more obedient to their masters than any other men in the world, be they religious or seculars; they show great respect to them nor do they lightly lie to them. They rarely or never contend with each other in word, and in action never. Fights, brawls, wounding, murder are never met with among them. Nor are robbers and thieves who steal on a large scale found there."

-Giovanni da Pian del Carpine

All in all, young Temujin's rise to power certainly was not an easy one. He had been deserted by most of his tribe. He was then attacked and chased mercilessly. He had survived, but reclaiming any semblance to the power that he once had would not be an easy task. This was demonstrated when he finally arrived at his mother's encampment, which he found to be deserted. He had no allies to find here, just an empty camp with nothing to offer but the ashes of long-dead fires and what seemed to be long-dead hopes.

Temujin would not give up, though. He had a hunch that his mother and siblings could not have gone far. He was right. He searched the surrounding area and found them hiding in nearby brush. This was, of course, a very smart thing to do since it was hard to tell if someone might later seek Hoelun out to exact vengeance, especially after all of the difficulty her son's enemies had experienced in trying to capture him.

[1] Hoang, Michel. *Genghis Khan*. 1988. Pg. 293.

At any rate, Temujin was able to locate his family, and they likely shared a heartfelt reunion with one another. Temujin was then able to lead his embattled relatives out of hiding to a nearby encampment of friendly tribal allies. They were safe for the time being, but survival still was not an easy prospect.

They only had a few horses. They also had very little food and were forced to mainly survive on trapping small critters, such as rabbits and squirrels, just to have a meal. Even more important than getting a bite to eat was the importance of making sure that they steered clear of trouble. There were still factions out there that would have liked to storm into their encampment and seize Temujin by force.

Temujin was in no position to fight them at this point, so it was his strategy to avoid them at all costs. At the same time, he did not want to drift too far from his kinsfolk since he had to keep his claim as khan alive. Temujin walked a tightrope in these early days, but he walked it well enough. He had been dealt a weak hand, but he learned to play it well. For the most part, he worked out a means of continued survival. However, there were still some obstacles ahead.

For instance, one morning, Temujin woke up to discover that the few horses he had to his name were all gone. Had they run away? Or even worse, did someone steal them in the middle of the night? As he looked around the camp, he happened upon a youngster and asked him if he had seen anything. The youth readily responded that he did. He saw some men come along and drive off the horses. He then offered to help Temujin find them.

His new friend was a man named Bo'orchu, who, in good time, would become one of his closest companions. With Bo'orchu in the lead, Temujin came upon the encampment that had taken possession of his stolen horses. The horses were right out in the open, tied up in a pasture. Still mindful of the weak hand he had to play, Temujin knew he was not ready to do battle with the horse thieves, so he simply tried to recover his horses without alerting them to his presence.

However, this was easier said than done since it is next to impossible to muffle the sound of a horse's hooves as they beat into the ground. And sure enough, as the pair left with the horses pounding away at the earth, Temujin and Bo'orchu were soon pursued by the horse thieves. These horse thieves (ironically enough) did not seem to want to be deprived of their stolen possessions.

Temujin's new friend Bo'orchu had a special surprise for their pursuers: arrows. Bo'orchu, as it turns out, was quite skilled at both horse riding and archery. He had the celebrated Mongolian skill of being able to ride a horse and then turn backward in the opposite direction while letting his arrows fly. Even as they made their mad dash away from their pursuers, he was able to fire off enough arrows to slow them down considerably. Bo'orchu also helped Temujin out further by leading him directly to his father's camp.

Unlike Temujin, this youngster was not an orphan. He had a father and a whole band of sympathetic warriors to tell the horse thieves to back off. It worked. The horse thieves realized that the jig was up. They finally relented and rode off in the other direction.

A statue of Bo'orchu. [a]

Temujin and Bo'orchu became fast friends, but Temujin had another friend in mind with whom he wanted to reacquaint himself. Just prior to Yesugei's passing, he had arranged for Temujin to be married to a young woman by the name of Borte. However, after the chaos that had erupted with his father's passing, he had lost track of his promised bride.

Temujin was determined to reconnect with her. A good bride, after all, was considered as good as gold in Mongolian relations since it connected the husband to her larger family structure and, therefore, offered him the support of more loyal kin.

In 1178, Temujin returned to Borte's village. Despite the years that had passed, Borte and her family received him warmly, recognizing the bond that had once been arranged between their clans. Though the exact details of what followed are lost to history, it is known that Temujin and Borte were soon married, officially sealing an alliance that would prove crucial to Temujin's rise.

Interestingly, in parts of eastern and central Asia today, echoes of these old marriage customs still survive. Among the Hmong people, for example, there is a custom known as bride pulling or wife catching—a symbolic and consensual act where the groom and his friends "abduct" the bride in a kind of playful ritual. The bride pretends to resist, and her relatives might snap photos, but everyone knows it is a performance. Afterward, the bride's family visits the groom's home, offering gifts and formally negotiating the marriage.

To a Western audience, this might seem odd or even awful, but within Hmong culture, it is viewed as a sweet, meaningful prelude to the wedding itself. It is tempting to imagine ancient ceremonies on the Mongol steppes carrying similar layers of symbolism. They were perhaps not the exact same, but modern traditions were likely built from the same cultural foundations of ritual, performance, and clan negotiation. While it is not known for certain if this happened at Temujin's wedding, it is very possible.

Temujin and Borte's ceremony would result in a tragic repeat of the misdeeds of the past. No sooner had the couple said "I do" than a raiding party stormed the encampment and snatched Borte away. This was certainly shocking, but those perpetrating the bride snatching were none other than the relatives of the man whom Temujin's mother, Hoelun, had been stolen from. Bizarrely enough, in the long-standing feuds of steppe culture, they were apparently waiting for this exact moment to carry out their revenge.

Of course, Temujin was not going to just sit back and allow such things to happen without a fight. He quickly got some of his best warriors together, and they rode off after the offending party. This was not a small operation. Some accounts suggest that he might have had as many as twenty thousand men accompany him on this quest.[i]

[i] Izzo, Robert. *The Life and Legend of Genghis Khan: Conquests, Power, Death, and the Mongol Empire.* 2020. Pg. 44.

These nomads lived life on the move, though, so it took some time to corner them. Temujin and his men ultimately found them, and they wasted no time in initiating a confrontation. Temujin prevailed against his foes, and he was able to rescue his bride. It was likely a touching scene, but one that was overshadowed by the obvious trauma that Borte had endured.

In fact, Borte gave birth nine months later. It was clearly understood that the baby was not Temujin's but rather the child of her captor, who had assaulted her while she was in his clutches. The child was given the name Jochi, which means "guest."[i] Even though the child was most likely not Temujin's, Temujin would go on to raise him as his own. He would also cherish his wife for the rest of his life.

[i] Izzo, Robert. *The Life and Legend of Genghis Khan: Conquests, Power, Death, and the Mongol Empire.* 2020. Pg. 52.

Chapter 3: Shoring Up Tribal Alliances and Temujin's Rise to Power

"Fair minded, with sound common sense. Remarkable well balanced; a good listener; a steadfast friend. Generous and affectionate; despite his sternness, having some fine qualities as an administrator, although by this must be understood the administration of nomadic peoples and not of settled populations. For theirs was an economy of which he had only a rather dim concept."

-Rene Grousset

The Mongolian steppes before Temujin's rise to power were fractured and chaotic, with tribes locked in endless cycles of rivalry. Such a disastrous state of chaos was beneficial for surrounding powers, most notably the Jin dynasty in China. As long as the Mongols remained divided, they would not pose an external threat. For decades, the Jin court deliberately encouraged this state of division, granting titles to some chieftains while withholding recognition from others just to keep the steppe fragmented. What Temujin accomplished was not merely the unification of tribes but also the overturning of a political balance that China had long relied upon for its security.

---

[1] Hoang, Michel. *Genghis Khan.* 1988. Pg. 288.

After consolidating his grip among his most loyal followers and solidifying his own personal family structure by marrying Borte, Temujin continued his rise to power. Interestingly, marriage had a lot to do with this. The more one married, the more tribal alliances one had, and the more profitable the marriage was deemed to be. The Mongolians of the Eurasian Steppe were well known for their polygamy. Temujin made brilliant use of this by marrying several different women, each of whom offered powerful strategic ties to influential clans.

His first and most significant union was with Borte of the Onggirat tribe, a respected and well-connected people. This bond gave Temujin legitimacy and an early foundation. Over the years, Borte bore Temujin several children, including Chagatai and Ogedei, both of whom would play major roles in the empire's future. These familial bonds formed the core of a new dynasty, even as Temujin's political ambitions continued to grow.

But marriage was just the beginning. His alliance-building soon expanded far beyond marital ties. One of his earliest and most important political moves was rekindling an old bond with Toghrul, the khan of the Keraits, who had once been a sworn brother (*anda*) to Temujin's father, Yesugei. To seal this renewed friendship, Temujin gifted Toghrul a sable cloak, a symbolic gesture that paid massive dividends. The Keraits were not just powerful. They were also known for their conversion to Nestorian Christianity, a rarity among the steppe tribes. The Keraits also wielded significant influence across central Mongolia.

A manuscript illustration of Genghis Khan and Toghrul.'

Toghrul likely needed the promise of Temujin's support just as much as Temujin craved his aid. The Keraits, though powerful, were constantly threatened by rival tribes on the steppe. The Naimans pressed in from the west, the Merkits harassed them from the north, and even the Tatars remained a lingering threat. Toghrul needed strong allies just to hold his position.

Then there was Jamukha, Temujin's childhood blood brother, a bond that was seen as sacred among the steppe peoples. The two shared a deep personal loyalty forged in youth, and in the early years of Temujin's rise, Jamukha stood by his side. Along with Toghrul, they joined forces in the daring campaign to rescue Borte after her abduction by the Merkit. This victory showcased Temujin's emerging ability to unite the different tribes under a shared banner.

But as their influence grew, so did their differences. Jamukha clung to the traditional aristocratic values of the steppe, such as noble lineage and elite control. Temujin, on the other hand, sought to elevate his loyal followers regardless of their birth. This ideological divide deepened with time and ultimately shattered their alliance.

Their first major clash came in 1187 at the Battle of Dalan Balzhut (Baljut), where Jamukha led a coalition of steppe nobles against Temujin's more modest, merit-based forces. Temujin was defeated, and Jamukha, asserting the old ways, brutally executed many of Temujin's captured soldiers by boiling them alive.

Yet, even after this, their rivalry continued. The death of Jamukha's brother, Taichar, in a skirmish with one of Temujin's men sparked a blood feud that made reconciliation impossible. In 1201, Jamukha was chosen as Gur-khan—"universal ruler"—by a confederation of tribes seeking to check Temujin's growing power.

However, the tide had turned. In the years that followed, Temujin outmaneuvered his rivals, winning key battles and absorbing enemy tribes into his growing confederation. By 1205, Jamukha had been betrayed by his own followers and handed over to Temujin. Rather than execute him cruelly, Temujin—perhaps honoring their bond as youths—granted him a swift and honorable death.

The arc of their relationship, from sworn brotherhood to deadly rivalry, mirrored the transformation of Mongol society itself. It was a struggle not just between two men but also between two visions of leadership: one rooted in birthright and the other in loyalty and merit.

As you can see, Temujin's path to unification was far from smooth. The early Mongolian landscape was full of shifting loyalties and rival khans. At times, Temujin's smaller forces were threatened by enemy coalitions many times their size. In such situations, he relied on what would become hallmarks of Mongolian warfare: mobility, flexibility, and psychological manipulation.

Though detailed records of Temujin's early battlefield tactics are sparse, it is widely accepted that he favored avoiding full-frontal engagements when possible. He understood the value of luring the enemy into overextending themselves. He would use feigned retreats and the terrain as tools. In later years, these tactics would become central to the Mongols' success.

An illustration of Genghis Khan.[5]

Stories passed down through Mongolian oral tradition speak of encampments being fortified under threat and of even noncombatants, including women, the elderly, and children, playing roles in defensive preparations. While it is difficult to verify the full extent of these actions, what is clear is that Temujin grasped the psychological power of perceived weakness. In battles where his enemies charged recklessly, they often met attacks from hidden flanks, ambushes from terrain thought empty, and volleys of arrows that turned confusion into chaos. Once the rout began, Mongolian horsemen gave no quarter. They pursued the enemy relentlessly and cut down fleeing opponents with terrifying efficiency.

Prisoners were sometimes taken, but often, the aftermath of a battle was as brutal as the fight itself. While accounts of Genghis Khan (or Temujin) boiling prisoners alive are not supported by credible sources and likely emerged from later exaggerations, acts of retribution and terror did occur, often as warnings to other would-be challengers.

Still, raw terror alone could not build an empire. Temujin understood that lasting power required loyalty, and loyalty was often earned through reward. One of his most effective policies was the division of plunder. After every victory, spoils were distributed equally among his troops. This broke with traditional aristocratic customs that prioritized noble lineages. Under Temujin's leadership, even low-born warriors could earn wealth and prestige. As word spread of his fairness and generosity, more tribes aligned themselves with him.

Among these groups was the Naimans, a major Turkic confederation in western Mongolia. They had once been formidable, but they were eventually defeated and incorporated into Temujin's growing coalition. The Uyghurs, renowned for their administrative skills and literacy, also pledged their allegiance, offering valuable bureaucratic talent. The Taichiud, a rival Mongol clan, eventually submitted as well, contributing notable commanders like Jebe, one of Temujin's most brilliant generals. The Ongud, a steppe people related by marriage to Temujin, became trusted vassals.

In 1203, everything nearly came crashing down for Temujin. The betrayal did not come from some distant enemy but from someone who had once been his greatest supporter: Toghrul, the Kerait khan. For years, Toghrul had acted as Temujin's patron and ally; he was almost like a second father. But the more Temujin's influence spread, the more suspicion took root. Persuaded by his son Senggum, Toghrul became convinced that Temujin was plotting to take his place.

The break came suddenly. Under the cover of a marriage celebration, Toghrul laid a trap. Temujin was warned just in time, and he escaped what could have been his end. The Battle of Khalkhaljid Sands took place soon after, and this time, Temujin's forces were overwhelmed. His men were cut down, and even his son Ogedei was left badly wounded. It looked like the dream of unifying the Mongols had died.

With only a handful of loyal followers left, Temujin retreated to the remote wilderness of Baljuna. There, things got so bad that the men drank muddy water mixed with horse blood just to stay alive. Yet instead of breaking them, this suffering forged them together. At Baljuna, Temujin and his remaining followers swore an oath known as the Baljuna Covenant. This was a promise that they would never abandon one another, no matter what. Those survivors, the Baljunatu, would become the hardened backbone of everything Temujin built afterward.

From what should have been the end, Temujin clawed his way back. Later that same year, he struck again. Toghrul and the Keraits fell. Toghrul died far from his throne, cut down by a Naiman soldier who did not even recognize him. Out of betrayal, disaster, and near ruin, Temujin had risen again. This time, nothing would stop Temujin from finishing what he had started.

By 1204, he had smashed the remaining resistance. In the Battle of Chakirmaut near the Altai foothills, he crushed a coalition of foes once thought unstoppable. With his enemies falling fast, Temujin created the Kheshig, an elite guard, and began reorganizing his forces into an efficient, loyal army. These men were more than just a war band; they were the bedrock of a new state.

In 1206, at a grand kurultai, or tribal council, on the sacred Burkhan Khaldun (one of the Khentii Mountains), the tribes assembled. Under the open sky, Temujin became Genghis Khan, "Universal Ruler," and with that title, he established the new Mongol Empire. It was a turning point not only for him but also for world history.

Burkhan Khaldun. [6]

A shaman named Kokochu presided over the sacred rites at the kurultai. Already regarded as Temujin's chief spiritual advisor, Kokochu emerged from the ceremony with new authority. Soon after, he proclaimed himself Teb Tengri, "the Most Heavenly One." In the world of the steppes, such a name carried immense weight. The Mongols believed that the eternal blue sky guided their destiny, and those who claimed to speak with its spirits commanded both reverence and fear.

Teb Tengri took full advantage of this. He began to speak not merely as a shaman but as if he were the divine mouthpiece of heaven itself. He held ceremonies in which he claimed to summon spirits and consult them on matters of state. When he spoke, many listened as though his words were revelations. Even Genghis Khan could not simply dismiss him. In those early years, the loyalty of tribes often rested as much on spiritual authority as on military might.

However, Teb Tengri's growing influence soon became dangerous. He began to turn his visions against the khan's own family, accusing his brother Kasar of secretly harboring ambitions to seize power. To ignore such warnings was perilous since many on the steppe believed that spirits revealed the truth through men. Genghis Khan, wary of dismissing what might be divine judgment, allowed suspicion to creep into his mind. For a time, Kasar's position was uncertain.

At one point, their mother, Hoelun, is said to have intervened. Hearing about the rising tensions, she rebuked her sons, reminding them that they were bound by blood and must not let the claims of a shaman drive them apart. For a while, her presence kept the peace. But when she passed away in the early 1210s, the family lost the one voice strong enough to command unity.

Without Hoelun, Teb Tengri pressed his advantage. He sought to expand his authority, demanding deference not only from common warriors but even from the khan's own brothers. The balance of power was tipping, and it became clear that the shaman intended to stand above all others. The khan's family would not simply submit. In a confrontation remembered in Mongol tradition, Kasar and Temuge seized Teb Tengri and brought him down by force, pulling the ropes of a tent upon him and killing him. Later accounts offer different versions of his fate. Some claim he was challenged to a wrestling match that turned deadly, while others say his spine was snapped.[i]

When news of this reached Genghis Khan, he made no move to punish them. Instead, he allowed the matter to pass in silence. It was a decision heavy with meaning. By letting Teb Tengri fall, Genghis Khan showed that no man—not even a shaman who claimed the voice of heaven—stood higher than the khan himself.

According to the *Secret History of the Mongols*, there was one final obstacle after Teb Tengri's death. His relatives, bound by custom, would have been expected to avenge him. On the steppe, such obligations were absolute. No matter how divisive or troublesome a man had been in life, his kin were honor-bound to strike back at those who killed him. To ignore such a duty risked shame, scorn, and the loss of standing among one's peers.

Yet Genghis Khan knew how to navigate this dangerous terrain. Instead of parading the body or leaving it in plain view, he ordered that Teb Tengri's corpse be hidden beneath a yurt. By doing this, his family could plausibly claim ignorance. If they had not "seen" the crime, they were not bound to answer it with blood. By covering the body, Genghis Khan covered the feud itself.

To modern readers, it may sound almost absurd that the simple act of concealing a body could dissolve such a sacred obligation. But in the harsh world of the steppe, such customs carried enormous weight. For

---

i Chambers, James. *Genghis Khan.* 2009. Pg. 90.

Teb Tengri's relatives, the hidden corpse offered an escape. They could avoid launching a blood feud they might not have wanted without losing honor. For Genghis Khan, it was a masterstroke of political calculation. He not only removed a rival but also prevented the cycle of vengeance that could have torn his fragile confederation apart.

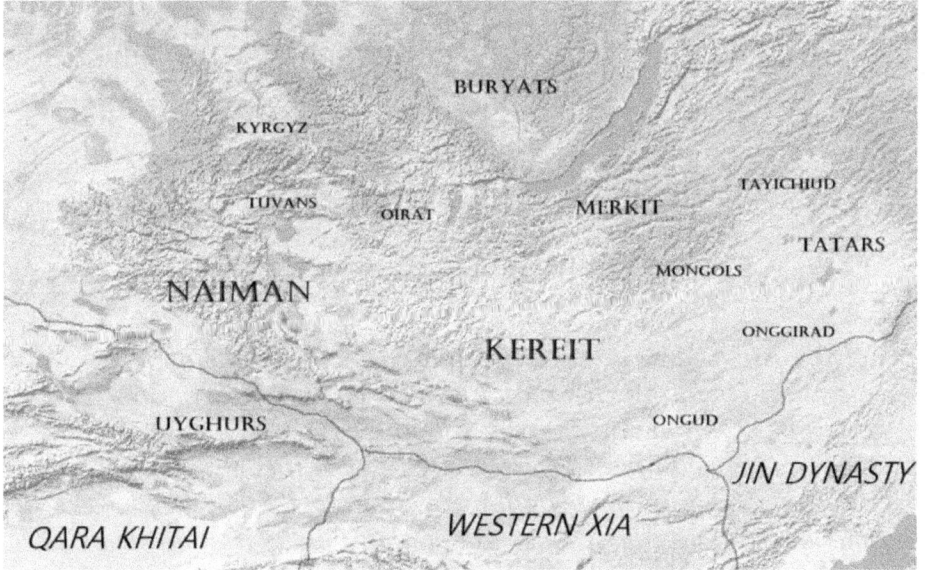

The Mongolian tribes that Genghis Khan united. '

Chapter 4: The Siege of Zhongdu

"Genghis Khan appears to us as the very embodiment of the steppe warrior with his instinct for the pragmatic and his inclination to plunder and despoil. Only by exceptional willpower did Genghis Khan succeed in reining in his instincts, in mastering them sufficiently to attain higher goals. Genghis distinguished himself invariably by his generosity, his magnanimity and his hospitality. But it is customary to represent Genghis Khan as a cruel despot, deceitful and vicious."

-Boris Vladimirtsov[i]

After 1206, with the steppe tribes united under his rule, Temujin—now Genghis Khan—turned his gaze outward. The most formidable neighbor was the Jurchen Jin dynasty, the rulers of northern China. The Jin had long dominated the steppe frontier, demanding tribute from Mongolian tribes in return for trade and nominal peace. In 1209, the throne passed to Wanyan Yongji, who inherited a vast empire stretching across Manchuria, Inner Mongolia, northern China, and even into Korea. Earlier Jin victories had driven the Song dynasty into southern China, leaving the north under Jurchen control. However, the empire was bloated. Inefficiency, corruption, and overreliance on walls and fortified cities had weakened them.

Yongji demanded that Genghis Khan, like his forefathers, submit and send tribute. The khan refused. Submission was incompatible with his vision. By rejecting Jin overlordship, Genghis Khan made open war inevitable.

[i] Hoang, Michel. *Genghis Khan*. 1988. Pg. 287.

Temujin being declared Genghis Khan.[8]

That war began in 1211. Gathering perhaps sixty thousand mounted warriors, Genghis Khan rode south toward the Jin frontier. The Jin had prepared by manning the Great Wall, particularly the Juyong Pass, north of their capital Zhongdu (modern Beijing). Yet the Great Wall, for all its imposing bulk, was too vast to defend everywhere at once. The Mongols broke through, slipping past the defenses with their hallmark speed and maneuverability.

Once inside Jin territory, Genghis Khan unleashed his armies with calculated precision. Scouts and light cavalry spread out, gathering intelligence and harassing the countryside. At Yehuling later that year, the Mongols faced a massive Jin army, perhaps 150,000 strong. As the Mongolian riders suddenly turned and fled, the Jin commanders, thinking victory was at hand, spurred their men forward in pursuit. But the Mongol retreat was no flight—it was a trap. Once the Jin had been drawn far from the safety of their fortified camps, the horsemen wheeled around with terrifying speed and struck. Panic spread through the Jin army. Their cavalry, desperate to turn back, crashed into their own infantry, trampling men underfoot. What had begun as an opportunity for triumph ended in slaughter. It was one of the most devastating defeats in Jin history.[i]

After the Battle of Yehuling, the war pressed deeper into Jin territory. Much of the fighting shifted toward fortified towns and strategic passes. One of the most decisive clashes came in the fall of 1211 at Huan'erzui, remembered as the Battle of Badger's Mouth. There, the Mongols faced a Jin army many times their size. Yet, numbers alone did not decide the day. Employing feigned retreats, sudden flanking maneuvers, and perfectly timed charges, Genghis Khan's riders broke the unity of their enemy. What began as a confident Jin advance turned into chaos, with cavalry trampling infantry and panic spreading across the field. The losses were staggering—it is reported that tens of thousands, perhaps more, died or were injured—but later claims of half a million dead are almost certainly exaggerations. What mattered was that the Jin's mighty forces were vulnerable to Mongol cunning.

The war did not end with a single victory. Through the harsh winter of 1211-12, Mongol forces pressed south, targeting fortified cities. One of their targets was Xijing, the western capital of the Jin (modern Datong). The defenders held firm, and during the fighting, Genghis Khan himself was struck by an arrow and badly wounded. With their leader injured and the stronghold proving too resilient, the Mongols were forced to pull back. For the Jin, it was a rare reprieve. For the Mongols, it was a reminder that their mastery of the open steppe did not guarantee success against stone walls.[ii]

[i] Chambers, James. *Genghis Khan*. 2009. Pg. 97.
[ii] Colwell Miller, Connie. *History's Biggest Disasters: The Biggest Military Battles*. 2018. Pg. 6.

In the years that followed, town after town fell. The Jin armies rarely ventured out from behind their walls, choosing to shelter in fortified cities. When they did engage, the results were disastrous.

Even so, Genghis Khan attempted to assure some of the besieged cities he encountered that he could be magnanimous. Smaller towns that surrendered were often spared, their officials were left in place, and their people were allowed to continue their lives under Mongol rule. In some cases, Buddhist and Daoist clergy even found favor with the khan. He valued their counsel and permitted them to keep their temples.

However, when cities resisted, the results were catastrophic. After the decisive Battle of Yehuling in 1211, captured Jin soldiers were cut down in staggering numbers. In 1212, when Xijing held out and Genghis Khan was wounded, the surrounding countryside was devastated in retribution. And in 1215, the great Jin capital of Zhongdu—modern Beijing—fell after a brutal siege. The Mongols stormed the city, unleashed a massacre, and set it ablaze. The destruction was so total that it spread terror across northern China, persuading other towns to surrender without resistance.

Genghis Khan was also willing to employ methods that horrified his enemies. One of his most notorious strategies was the use of prisoners of war as unwilling shock troops. Captives were driven before the Mongol ranks, forced to fill in ditches, haul siege engines, or simply march against city walls under a hail of arrows. For defenders looking out from their battlements, the sight was appalling. Their missiles struck not hardened Mongol warriors but their own people who had been pressed into service as living shields.

This strategy of "mercy for the obedient, destruction for the rebellious" became one of Genghis Khan's most effective tools of conquest. It explains why some remember him as a surprisingly tolerant ruler who allowed freedom of worship and upheld treaties, while others see only the devastation he left in his wake.

After Genghis Khan was injured at Xijing in 1212, operations slowed, but the Mongols did not retreat. Instead, Genghis Khan took the time to rethink his strategy. The fierce resistance of Jin fortresses convinced him of the need for skilled engineers. He began recruiting defectors—Chinese and Jin specialists in siege warfare—who brought with them the knowledge of catapults, siege towers, and other technologies the nomads had never used before.

This shift revealed the deep weakness of the Jin dynasty. Divisions within their empire left many ready to defect, and Genghis Khan skillfully exploited this disunity. Over the next several years, his newly equipped forces broke through key fortresses, eventually pushing past the defenses of the Juyong Pass, the main gateway to Zhongdu.

Before the siege of Zhongdu reached its climax, the Jin dynasty was unraveling from within. The Khitans, once subjects of the Jin, rose in rebellion, providing aid to the Mongols and striking at Jin authority. Then, in 1213, a coup toppled Emperor Wanyan Yongji, replacing him with Xuanzong, a move that only deepened the dynasty's instability.

For the Mongols, who had already advanced deep into northern China, this internal chaos was a stroke of fortune. Genghis Khan knew his forces were overstretched and that prolonged siege warfare drained his strength. When his army encircled Zhongdu in 1214, he agreed to a truce. The terms were extraordinarily favorable. Tribute poured out of the Jin capital in the form of gold, silk, horses, and even a princess. For a moment, the siege was lifted, and the Mongols withdrew north.

However, the reprieve was short-lived. Emperor Xuanzong, convinced that Zhongdu was indefensible, moved his court south to Kaifeng. To Genghis Khan, this was both a betrayal of the treaty and a clear sign that the Jin were preparing for renewed resistance. The khan resolved that the Jin dynasty would not be allowed to recover.

Genghis Khan mobilized his army once again. In late 1214, the Mongols returned to Zhongdu and laid siege to the city. The Mongols encircled the capital, cutting off all supplies. Inside the walls, famine soon reached horrifying extremes. According to Chinese sources, the shortage of food became so desperate that the inhabitants resorted to cannibalism. Relief armies sent by Emperor Xuanzong were repeatedly intercepted and destroyed by the Mongols before they could reach the city.

As months dragged on, the defenders' morale collapsed. When the city's commanders tried to rally one last offensive, their soldiers refused. Some officials surrendered. Others chose suicide over capture. By summer 1215, the resistance had crumbled. The gates were opened, and Zhongdu fell to the Mongols.

The Mongols showed little mercy. Once the walls were breached, the city was engulfed in fire, and a great slaughter followed. Thousands of inhabitants were cut down, while those who survived saw their possessions seized as plunder for the victors. Chinese chronicles describe streets full of corpses, and later observers claimed that the very ground seemed to carry the stain of the massacre.[i]

Reports of the destruction spread far beyond China. Diplomats and merchants who passed through the ruins carried tales of horror back to central Asia, reinforcing the Mongols' reputation for ruthless conquest. Whether or not every detail was true, the message was unmistakable: resistance to Genghis Khan meant annihilation.

---

[i] Chambers, James. *Genghis Khan.* 2009. Pg. 103.

Chapter 5: The Fall of the Khwarazmian Empire

"Under the reign of Genghis Khan, all of the country between Iran and Turan enjoyed such peace that one could travel from east to west with a golden tray upon one's head without being subjected to the slightest hint of violence from anyone."

-Abul-Ghazi

If Genghis Khan had wished to destroy the Jin dynasty, he could have, but Genghis Khan's intent was mainly to humble them and end any potential uprising. Once this had been accomplished, he returned to his base of operations in Mongolia and turned his mind to other things. The Jin would cling to power until 1234 when Genghis Khan's successors finally put them out of business for good.

After the Mongols humbled the Jin, the Mongols began to turn their sights toward the mighty Islamic conglomerate known as the Khwarazmian Empire. This empire consisted of Afghanistan and Persia (modern-day Iran). It had been forged after the rise of Islam in the 7th century. It must be noted that the Persians were unwilling partners in all of this. They had been forcibly conquered and made to convert from their traditional faith of Zoroastrianism to Islam.

By the time of Genghis Khan, the Khwarazmian Empire stretched across much of Central Asia, from the Oxus River to the Persian

---

[1] Hoang, Michel. *Genghis Khan.* 1988. Pg. 294.

heartlands. It controlled the caravan routes and wealthy trading cities that linked China with the Islamic world. Its ruler, Sultan Muhammad II, had inherited a powerful realm from his father, Tekish, and he harbored ambitions of making himself the supreme power of the Islamic world. He dreamed of replacing the weakened Abbasid caliph in Baghdad as the true leader of the faithful. Genghis Khan, for his part, did not initially see Muhammad as an enemy. In fact, he looked upon the Khwarazmian Empire as a potential partner—a western counterpart to his growing dominion in the east.

Sometime around 1218, after the defeat of the Jin in northern China, Genghis Khan sent an embassy westward. The mission was designed to open diplomatic and commercial relations between the two powers. At its head was a group of Mongol merchants and Muslim traders from Central Asia, who carried with them fine goods, including silk, furs, and other luxury items, meant for the bustling markets of Khwarazmian cities like Otrar, Bukhara, and Samarkand. Genghis Khan also sent along a personal message, one that modern historians still debate in tone. Some chronicles say that the khan spoke to Sultan Muhammad with an air of respect, referring to him as a "brother" and offering peace between equals. Others record that Genghis used more authoritative language, boasting of his conquests and subtly suggesting that the sultan was his junior. The main thing that Genghis Khan wanted to establish with this message was creating an open trade route and formalizing ties.

For a brief moment, it seemed as if a great partnership might take root. The idea of a Mongolian-Khwarazmian Silk Road that carried goods across Asia promised wealth for both sides. However, such hopes did not last. Suspicion and mistrust clouded the sultan's court. Sultan Muhammad had already heard stories of Genghis Khan's devastating campaigns against the Jin and other neighbors. He did not trust that this rising nomad king truly sought peace.

When the Mongol merchants arrived in the border city of Otrar, disaster struck. The city's governor, Inalchuq (also called Ghayir Khan), accused the merchants of being spies. It was not an unfounded fear. The Mongols had indeed used merchants and travelers in the past to gather intelligence. But in this case, they had come under a flag of safe conduct. Inalchuq ignored this. Acting on his own authority—though some say he did so with the sultan's tacit approval—he ordered the entire caravan seized. The goods were confiscated, and the men were killed.

When word reached Genghis Khan, he was stunned and enraged. This was not merely an insult; it was an outright violation of the sacred law of envoys and guests, a principle respected across the steppe and the Islamic world alike. Still, the khan did not immediately declare war. He sent another official embassy to the sultan, demanding an explanation and punishment for Inalchuq. Three envoys were dispatched. One was a Mongol, and the other two were Muslim merchants. They were chosen deliberately so that Muhammad could not claim bias. However, when they arrived, the sultan had the Mongol envoy executed and the two Muslim ambassadors humiliated. Their beards were shaved, and their faces were mutilated. Then, they were sent back east. It was one of the gravest insults possible.

The message was clear. Sultan Muhammad would not treat with the Mongols on equal terms. Upon hearing how his envoys had been slaughtered and shamed, Genghis Khan is said to have stood before his followers and declared that no greater crime could be committed between rulers. It was, in his mind, not only an insult but a betrayal of sacred customs.

From that moment forward, the khan's mind turned entirely to war. He was in his late fifties, and he was already the master of a vast empire stretching from the forests of Siberia to the Yellow River. But this new challenge was unlike those before. The Khwarazmian Empire was no minor kingdom. It was a sprawling dominion, rich in resources, peopled by hardened warriors, and ruled by a sultan who believed himself the heir to Alexander the Great. For many rulers, such a task would have seemed impossible. But for Genghis Khan, it was the very test he relished.

In the winter of 1218-19, he began preparing. The Mongolian army was divided into four great tumens (a military or administrative unit consisting of ten thousand soldiers or people), each commanded by a trusted son or general. Jochi, his eldest son, was given the northern route, pressing through the steppes and deserts toward the Aral Sea. Chagatai and Ogedei, the second and third sons, marched together through the central approach, striking at the great cities along the Syr Darya. Subutai, a brilliant general, was unleashed in another direction. He was tasked with sweeping the flanks and harassing enemy strongholds. Genghis Khan himself would march at the center of it all, bearing down upon the richest jewel of the Khwarazmian world: Bukhara.

This was no rash invasion. Every detail was accounted for. Supplies were stockpiled, herds of horses were prepared for the long campaign, and intelligence was gathered with ruthless efficiency. Scouts rode ahead across the deserts of Transoxiana, mapping rivers, wells, and caravan trails. Local chieftains along the frontier were bribed or threatened into cooperation, ensuring the Mongols would not lack guides. Even before the first arrow flew, the khan had already set in motion one of the most carefully orchestrated invasions of the medieval world.

The mutilated envoys did not disappear into the shadows of history. When Genghis Khan addressed his troops before the campaign, he pointed to the surviving ambassadors, their disfigurements still fresh. "Look upon them," he is said to have declared. "This is what the Khwarazmian Empire has done. He has struck at your brothers, your khan, and the Eternal Blue Sky itself. We go now to demand justice."

By the spring of 1219, the preparations were complete. Riders fanned out across the steppes, calling men to arms. From the Altai Mountains to the shores of Lake Balkhash and from the forests of Siberia to the Gobi Desert, warriors gathered. Tens of thousands assembled, hardened from years of conquest in China and the steppes. The khan rode among them, promising them not only victory but also the spoils of the richest lands they had ever seen. Silk, gold, and jewels awaited them. More importantly, honor awaited them—the chance to avenge their khan's dishonor.

The Mongols crossed the Jaxartes River and thundered into Khwarazmian lands. For Sultan Muhammad II, the storm he had unleashed was about to break with a fury unlike any the Islamic world had seen since the days of the first Arab conquests. Genghis Khan entrusted each division to a son or trusted general, so that no matter what path the Khwarazmians chose, a Mongol hammer would be waiting.

Jochi, his eldest, pushed southward. His orders were to harry and draw out the enemy rather than waste lives in a pitched battle. This was a tactic the Mongols had perfected against the Jin, and it was meant to break the sultan's nerve without ever giving him the satisfaction of a decisive engagement.

At first, Jochi's forces executed the plan flawlessly. They struck supply trains, scattered small detachments, and vanished again into the emptiness of the steppe. Their arrows cut down isolated companies before the enemy even had time to unsheathe a sword. Then, when the Khwarazmian host finally lumbered into motion, Jochi and his men would melt away, leaving their exhausted foe chasing shadows across the plain.

However, over time, his men grew restless. They had tasted victory in northern China and seen whole armies collapse before them. Some began to grumble that their commander was too cautious. They did not think they should flee before an enemy they could beat.

The Khwarazmian sultan, meanwhile, gathered strength. Eventually, Jochi's band of raiders came into contact with the main body of Muhammad's army. This was no scattered garrison force; it was the sultan's personal host, thick with cavalry and hardened by years of border wars against restless tribes.

The clash was brutal. Chroniclers say that some of Jochi's captains urged him to retreat, warning that the enemy outnumbered them by a vast margin. But Jochi—perhaps eager to prove himself to his father or perhaps unwilling to let his younger brothers outshine him—insisted they stand. His warriors thundered headlong into the Khwarazmian flank, loosing arrows at point-blank range as they closed. One entire wing of the sultan's army buckled and fell back. For a fleeting moment, it seemed the Mongols might rip through the line entirely. Some even claimed that the sultan himself, Muhammad II, came within the range of Jochi's archers. Showers of arrows fell about his person, forcing him to break off and ride to the rear.

But if the Mongols thought this would shatter the Khwarazmian force, they were mistaken. The sultan's son, Jalal al-Din, seized command, rallying the wavering soldiers and hurling them back into the fight. His energy and fury steadied the line, and soon, the Mongols found themselves pressed hard. Their numbers could not stand in a prolonged clash. Reluctantly, Jochi gave the order to withdraw.

It was a bloody retreat, but it was not a defeat in the ordinary sense. Though Jalal al-Din had forced the Mongols to yield the field, the sultan had paid dearly. Tens of thousands of his men lay dead, trampled under horses or hit by Mongol arrows. It was a victory bought at such a ruinous cost that it weakened rather than strengthened Khwarazmian power.

Genghis Khan, watching from afar as reports came in, must have understood the deeper meaning. The Khwarazmians were strong in numbers, but they could not endure such losses forever. The sultan had shown that he would bleed himself dry for the appearance of triumph. And unlike the Jin, who could retreat into fortified cities and vast hinterlands, Muhammad's empire depended on keeping its armies intact to shield its many subject peoples. Each costly "victory" only paved the way for collapse.

While Jochi and the others struck blows at the edges, Genghis Khan himself drove into the heart of the Khwarazmian dominion. His target was Bukhara, the famed jewel of Transoxiana. For centuries, it had stood as a crossroads of the Silk Road, a seat of Islamic scholarship, and a prize every conqueror longed to claim. To take Bukhara was to tear a hole into the sultan's prestige.

In early 1220, the Mongols appeared on its doorstep. However, their approach was not the plodding march of a conventional army. Rather than pushing through the usual mountain passes, Genghis Khan took the unthinkable route across the Kyzylkum Desert (modern Uzbekistan). For days, his men and horses trudged through the burning sands, guided only by captured locals and the discipline of a people who had grown up in harsh steppe landscapes. It was a march so bold that Muhammad II never considered it possible. He expected the Mongols to filter down through the valleys of the Syr Darya; instead, they materialized like phantoms before Bukhara's walls.

The city, though famed for its scholars, was not prepared to resist such a storm. The main garrison had already been drawn away by the sultan to face the northern Mongol attacks, leaving only a skeleton force inside. According to Persian chronicler Juvayni, when the gates were breached, the defenders were too stunned to mount a serious resistance.

Yet Genghis Khan staged the assault with his usual cold calculation. He stationed men before every gate of the city save one. This "unguarded" gate was no accident; it was bait. When a force of some twenty thousand troops sallied forth—many of them mercenaries hired to stiffen the defense—they found the way open. They charged out as though to smash through the besiegers, only to wheel aside in a feigned assault and scatter across the plain.

The Mongols let them go—for a day. Then, like wolves circling stray sheep, they tracked the fleeing army to the banks of a river. Exhausted, leaderless, and with nowhere to run, the mercenaries were cut down.

Inside the city, the drama played out differently. The imams and scholars of Bukhara, fearing slaughter, went out to meet the conqueror.

When Genghis Khan entered, he is said to have gone first to a mosque, where he addressed the assembled people. Chroniclers put words in his mouth that were as much theater as threat: "I am the punishment of God. If you had not committed great sins, God would not have sent a punishment like me upon you."

Of course, it is not known for sure whether he spoke those exact words. But it was still clear that the pagan conqueror from the steppes had set foot in Islam's holy space and was bending the city not only by arms but also by awe.

The governor of Bukhara, meanwhile, retreated with his household troops into the citadel. Even after the outer city surrendered, he held out stubbornly, barricading himself in the fortress at the center. But the Mongols, who had reduced Chinese strongholds far stronger than this, set to work with siege engines and fire. Within days, the walls cracked, and the citadel fell.

Bukhara was Genghis Khan's now. Its craftsmen were spared. They were sent eastward to enrich the Mongol homeland with their skills. Its treasures were stripped and divided among the soldiers. Its defenders who had resisted were slain. And its people were left in no doubt that the storm breaking over the Khwarazmian Empire was unstoppable.

If Bukhara had been a jewel of the Silk Road, Samarkand was its crown. It was more populous, more fortified, and more renowned. It basically stood as the beating heart of the Khwarazmian Empire. Whoever held Samarkand commanded the arteries of trade, making them the most powerful in the region. Genghis Khan knew that striking it swiftly while the sultan was on the run would shatter Khwarazmian authority across the region.

In the spring of 1220, the Mongol host appeared before its walls. The city was better defended than Bukhara. Muhammad II had stationed a large garrison there. Chroniclers estimate anywhere from 40,000 to 100,000 men were there, though medieval numbers should always be treated with caution. The defenders also had war elephants that had been brought from India. To any ordinary invader, this would have been daunting. However, Genghis Khan and his generals pressed forward with the same measured ferocity as before.

The Mongols set up a blockade around the city, cutting Samarkand off from reinforcements. Siege engines, including stone-throwers, catapults, and scaling towers, were assembled from timber brought along the march or seized locally. Genghis also employed his signature tactic: sowing fear and confusion. Small Mongol units galloped around the walls day and night, loosing arrows, setting fires, and luring sorties into ambush.

When the elephants were unleashed, the Mongols answered with volleys of flaming arrows. The beasts panicked and trampled their own lines, sowing chaos in the Khwarazmian ranks. This collapse of order gave the Mongols the opening they needed. One gate after another buckled under sustained assault, and the disciplined steppe warriors poured through.

What followed was the kind of catastrophe that would make Samarkand's name a byword for ruin. Entire quarters of the city were set ablaze. The citadel, like Bukhara's before it, was besieged. Its garrison was stubborn, but it was doomed. According to Juvayni, tens of thousands were slaughtered, though the exact number will never be known. What is clear is that those who resisted were annihilated.

Yet, as always, the Mongols tempered destruction with pragmatism. Skilled artisans, smiths, and craftsmen were rounded up and spared. They were sent east to Karakorum and other Mongol centers to enrich the empire with their knowledge. Scholars were also sometimes spared since Genghis Khan recognized the value of record keepers and administrators. However, the common people, for the most part, paid dearly.

For Muhammad II, the fall of Samarkand was a disaster. From Samarkand, Genghis sent detachments that fanned out across the empire. The sultan's power was broken, but the Mongols would not stop until every fortress, every city, and every corner of the Khwarazmian dominion bent to their will.

The capture of Samarkand was more than a military triumph; it was a psychological earthquake. One of the greatest cities of the Islamic world had fallen not after years of siege but in mere weeks. Rumors spread like wildfire. People said that the Mongols were invincible, that their armies were numberless, and that resistance was hopeless. Panic gripped the Khwarazmian domains, and the people began to turn against Sultan Muhammad, the man who had once dreamed of rivaling the caliph himself.

Instead of rallying his forces for a last stand, Sultan Muhammad chose to flee. Historians have long criticized this decision. In the summer of 1220, as Samarkand's walls crumbled, Muhammad II fled westward. At first, he lingered in the region of Balkh, perhaps hoping to regroup, but Mongol detachments moved too swiftly.

Among these pursuers were two of the khan's greatest generals, Jebe and Subutai. These commanders were already veterans of countless campaigns, and they were unleashed like hounds to find the sultan.

So, Sultan Muhammad's flight became one of desperation. He moved through northern Iran and then toward the Caspian coast. He never stayed too long in one place. Chroniclers note that he disguised himself, traveling in small retinues. He often concealed himself among caravans. His people, already terrorized by the Mongols, likely looked upon him with growing suspicion. Why should they risk dying for a man who would not risk his own life to defend them?

Everywhere he went, Mongol scouts followed close behind. Subutai and Jebe were relentless. They covered astonishing distances with their light cavalry, spreading terror as they pressed deeper into Persia. Cities that might have sheltered the sultan closed their gates because governors feared Mongol reprisal if they harbored him.

At last, Sultan Muhammad sought refuge on an island in the Caspian Sea, near modern-day Turkmenistan. He arrived there broken in spirit. He had been stripped of his authority, with only a few loyal retainers at his side. It was a hard exile for a man who had once commanded one of the richest empires in the Islamic world.

In December 1220, wracked with illness—some sources say pleurisy, others simply call it a fever—Sultan Muhammad II died. He was only in his mid-forties, a man still in his prime by the standards of kingship. Yet his empire lay in ruins. His people had abandoned him (and vice versa), and his sons were left to inherit the disaster.

In the meantime, the Mongols turned their attention to the city of Khujand, which is today in modern Tajikistan. Though the city itself fell quickly, its governor, Timur Malik, refused to submit. With roughly a thousand loyal troops, he withdrew to a fortified island in the Syr Darya River, which cut through the city. From this stronghold, he defied the Mongols, harrying their positions and forcing them to engage in a long, bitter struggle. His stand became legendary, though in the end, the island was stormed. There are no more mentions of Timur Malik in the chronicles, so it is assumed he died in the assault.[i]

His death did not end the Mongols' pursuit. Genghis Khan ordered the hunt to continue, this time against Muhammad's heir, Jalal al-Din. The younger man was cut from a different cloth than his father, and his defiance would give the Mongols one of their fiercest fights.

At just twenty-something years of age, Jalal al-Din had found himself thrust into leadership. However, he obviously did not inherit a strong empire. Cities lay in ruins, his armies were scattered, and the Mongols pressed relentlessly westward. Yet, in the midst of all this disaster, Jalal al-Din resolved to resist.

By early 1221, he had gathered a loyal core of troops in Persia and then in Afghanistan. Despite the crushing Mongol onslaught, he was able to rally local commanders, tribal warriors, and remnants of his father's army. His cause gained strength, not only because of his courage but also because he symbolized the last hope of defiance against the invaders. Unlike Muhammad II, Sultan Jalal al-Din was willing to share the hardships of his men. He rode at the head of the army, ate the same food, and slept on the same ground.

However, the Mongols were not about to allow his resistance to grow unchecked. Genghis Khan, still in his prime as a warlord, personally took the field against him. The khan, who was accompanied by Subutai and other trusted commanders, pursued Jalal al-Din across Afghanistan. Skirmishes broke out in valleys and mountain passes. Time and time again, Jalal al-Din's forces were driven back, but they were never annihilated. Each retreat bought him time, and each stand bloodied the Mongols just enough to show that he was not going to be as easy a mark as his father.

At last, in the spring of 1221, Jalal al-Din made a bold stand on the banks of the Indus River, near what is now Pakistan. Here, cut off from retreat, he chose to fight rather than yield. His army, numbering perhaps thirty thousand men, faced a Mongol force at least twice that size. On the open plain, the odds were hopeless. Yet Jalal rallied his warriors with fiery words, declaring that it was better to die with honor than live in humiliation.

---

[i] Chambers, James. *Genghis Khan*. 2009. Pg. 113.

The battle that followed was fierce. Jalal al-Din's cavalry charged with desperate valor, breaking through the Mongol lines more than once. Genghis Khan himself is said to have watched from a rise, astonished by the young prince's audacity. For hours, the fight raged. Mongol arrows darkened the sky, horses charged, and the Indus River ran red with blood.

At last, the weight of the Mongols' numbers began to show. Jalal al-Din's men were cut down in heaps. The river loomed behind them, offering no escape. Yet in the moment of his greatest peril, Jalal al-Din performed the deed that would make his name legendary. Spurring his horse, he plunged straight into the Indus River. With arrows whistling all around him, he and a small band of followers swam their mounts across the raging current to safety on the far bank.

Jalal al-Din crossing the Indus River.[9]

From the opposite shore, Jalal al-Din turned to face the Mongols once more. He raised his arm defiantly, signaling that though beaten, he was not broken. Genghis Khan witnessed this spectacle and is said to have remarked that a father who had fled like a coward had somehow produced a son who was a lion. He forbade his men from shooting any more arrows, choosing instead to admire his foe.

Jalal al-Din's escape did not save his empire—it was already in ashes—but it did carve him a place in history. He spent the next years as a fugitive king, wandering across India. He later returned west, still harassing the Mongol forces where he could. Though his reign was short and filled with hardship, his defiance at the Indus River stood as one of the rare moments when the Mongols were forced to acknowledge the valor of an enemy.

By the early 1230s, Jalal al-Din's cause had crumbled, and he met his death at the hands of Kurdish assassins. His fall marked the last flicker of Khwarazmian resistance to the Mongols.

Nevertheless, the Mongols had secured the Silk Road and a huge swathe of territory in the process. For the Mongols, such things were certainly worthy of celebration. The Silk Road had long been under the control of powerful Chinese dynasties, but the turbulence of external forces had pressured the Chinese to curtail their use of the once wide-ranging trade routes. First, the Jin had seized northern China, pushing the Song dynasty into the south. The Song dynasty tried to make the best of a bad situation by playing the Jin against the Mongols. It was hoped that the two would wear each other out fighting each other and leave southern China alone.

However, after the Mongols defeated the Jin and gained control of the coveted Silk Road, the Mongol Empire became a greater threat to the Southern Song dynasty, more so than the Jin ever were. The Jin had been so preoccupied in its struggle against the Southern Song dynasty that it never really established control over the Silk Road.

The Mongols were quick to consolidate their control over the trade routes. Considering as much, it could be argued that, strategically speaking, the Mongols had better-placed priorities than the Jin did. Rather than immediately taking the fight to the Southern Song, the Mongols took their time in consolidating the territory already under their control—territory that now included the Silk Road.

Before his rise, the famed Silk Road was less a road than a patchwork of risky trails connecting east and west. Caravans carrying precious goods like silk, jade, glassware, and spices constantly faced the threat of ambush. Rival steppe tribes, squabbling warlords, and opportunistic bandits made long-distance trade a gamble of life and death.

Genghis Khan changed that dynamic in a dramatic fashion. Once he had subdued central Asia, his armies brought a measure of stability to lands that had been fractured for centuries. Banditry, once a plague on merchants, was ruthlessly stamped out. The khan's law code, the Yassa, carried severe punishments for theft and violence against travelers. This meant that merchants could cross vast stretches of central Asia under the promise of protection.

Another one of Genghis Khan's great innovations was his communication network, known to history as the yam system. The Mongols had always relied on mounted messengers to carry news across the steppe. Traditionally, a single rider on a fast horse would deliver urgent news to the nearest encampment. From there, another rider on a fresh horse would continue the message to the next camp, and so on, until the word had spread across hundreds of miles. Genghis Khan did not invent this, but he did expand it into something vast and unprecedented.

Genghis Khan's empire stretched thousands of miles, and keeping it connected was as important as winning any battle. To solve the problem, he established a chain of relay stations, each about twenty-five to thirty miles apart—the distance a horse could gallop at full speed before tiring. At each post, fresh horses and riders were kept at the ready. A messenger could thunder into a station, hand off the message, and within moments, a new rider would already be racing off to the next station. Using this system, messages could travel as far as two hundred miles in a single day—an astonishing speed for the medieval world.

This system allowed Genghis Khan to exercise direct control over even the most distant corners of his empire. Orders could reach generals in weeks instead of months. News of rebellion, invasion, or opportunity could be delivered swiftly back to the khan. The yam system was not just for war. It also carried intelligence, diplomatic messages, and even trade goods. Travelers and envoys who carried official credentials, called paiza, could expect food, shelter, and new mounts at the waystations, which doubled as inns and supply posts.

This system was so effective that later writers compared it to the Pony Express of 19ᵗʰ-century America, where fresh riders and horses carried mail across the frontier. In fact, some historians even view the modern postal service as a descendant of these steppe traditions. Like the Pony Express, the yam system was built on speed, efficiency, and the endurance of both man and horse. But in scale, the Mongol system far surpassed anything the world had seen before.

The yam system was another tool of imperial control. It stitched together an empire that spanned from the Pacific to the Black Sea, creating an artery through which orders, intelligence, and ideas flowed. Combined with Genghis Khan's legal code and his protection of merchants along the Silk Road, the yam system helped transform the Mongol domains from a loose confederation of tribes into a functioning imperial system.

Historians later described this period as the Pax Mongolica—the Mongol Peace. Under its shadow, the Silk Road flourished in ways it had not since the glory days of the Tang dynasty. The flow of silk, porcelain, and tea from China, as well as glass, textiles, and perfumes from Persia and beyond, reached unprecedented levels. More than material goods traveled along these routes. Ideas, technologies, and even diseases moved as never before. Paper-making and printing spread westward. Islamic medicine and mathematics reached China. But so, too, did the Black Death, the plague that would devastate Eurasia in the mid-14ᵗʰ century.

The origins of the plague lay in the wild rodent populations of central Asia. Long before Europeans had even heard of it, outbreaks were already moving silently along the caravan trails of the steppe. With the Mongols in command of a vast, interconnected empire, the plague found new highways to travel. Traders, soldiers, and envoys carried the bacteria with them, often unknowingly.

One of the most chilling episodes came in 1346 at the Crimean port city of Caffa. Here, the Mongol Golden Horde besieged the city, which was then held by Genoese merchants. Midway through the siege, the plague broke out among the Mongol ranks. According to Italian accounts, the Mongols hurled infected corpses over the walls in an early act of biological warfare. Whether or not this gruesome tactic was the true cause, the defenders soon found themselves stricken by the same disease. Many of the Genoese fled by ship, carrying the plague westward across the Mediterranean. Within a year, the disease had erupted in Sicily, and from there, it spread across Europe like wildfire.

The results were catastrophic. Between 1347 and 1351, the Black Death ravaged Europe, killing anywhere from one-third to over half the population. Entire towns vanished, economies collapsed, and the social fabric of Europe was permanently altered. None of this was what Genghis Khan had intended when he forged his empire. Yet the Mongol achievement of connecting distant civilizations made the rapid spread of the Black Death possible.

The Mongols had opened the doors of Eurasia to trade and cultural exchange, but in doing so, they had also opened the door to one of the deadliest pandemics in human history.

Chapter 6: Warfare and Strategy

"Genghis Khan and his line were guilty of no particular taste for murder, nor of sadism, nor of any highly developed penchant for cruelty. They were merely exceptionally well-organized barbarians who carried a system to its farthest limits. They waged war because it was their natural state to be either murderers or victims. One might compare their actions to those of a power that possess the atom bomb and is determined to use it. They were, however, in no fear of reprisals since they had no cities. They were not particularly wicked but merely served their own interests first and foremost."

-Jean Paul Roux[i]

Even though the Khwarazmian Empire had been laid to waste, the Mongol leader, Genghis Khan, was not satisfied. Sultan Muhammad II had escaped, and Genghis Khan wanted to track him down and capture him. He ordered his general Subutai to do just that. Subutai and his men led a search party. They eventually tracked the sultan to Nishapur.

It must be mentioned that Genghis Khan and his forces exacted what can only be termed as a rather remarkable revenge on this city. Genghis Khan and his troops almost always employed brutal and heavy-handed tactics, but the way they waged war on Nishapur was even more extreme than usual. The reason? Just prior to this assault, one of Genghis Khan's sons-in-law had perished in a skirmish with this city. Genghis Khan's daughter was deeply saddened by the loss of her husband. Genghis Khan apparently thought he could make amends for his daughter by

---

[i] Hoang, Michel. *Genghis Khan*. 1988. Pgs. 288-289.

exacting one of the most extreme forms of vengeance he ever perpetuated. He made sure to give his daughter a front-row seat, having her ride behind thousands of Mongol troops. This was highly unusual since women did not usually get this close to the front lines.

Once they broke through the city gates, they killed everything that moved. It is said that they killed men, women, children, and even dogs and cats. Yes, even the family pets were not safe once the Mongols were in town. The Mongols chopped off the heads of the dead, which they then stacked in grisly piles.

The sultan was always one step ahead and had already slipped away, doing so just before this onslaught was unleashed. He fled north to the city of Kazvin.

By this point, Sultan Muhammad II had lost almost his entire army. He was flanked only by his most loyal guards. The sultan was so paranoid that he barely even trusted his own guards. He slept in a different tent every night just in case some would-be opportunist from within his inner circle decided to seize him and drag him off to Genghis Khan.

Genghis Khan's general Subutai made sure to keep the sultan on his toes, relentlessly following him from town to town. Right when they nearly had him in their sights, Sultan Muhammad managed to board a boat and flee across the Caspian Sea to the island of Abaskun. Even though he escaped capture, he died the following year on January 10th, 1221. He died a king without a kingdom.

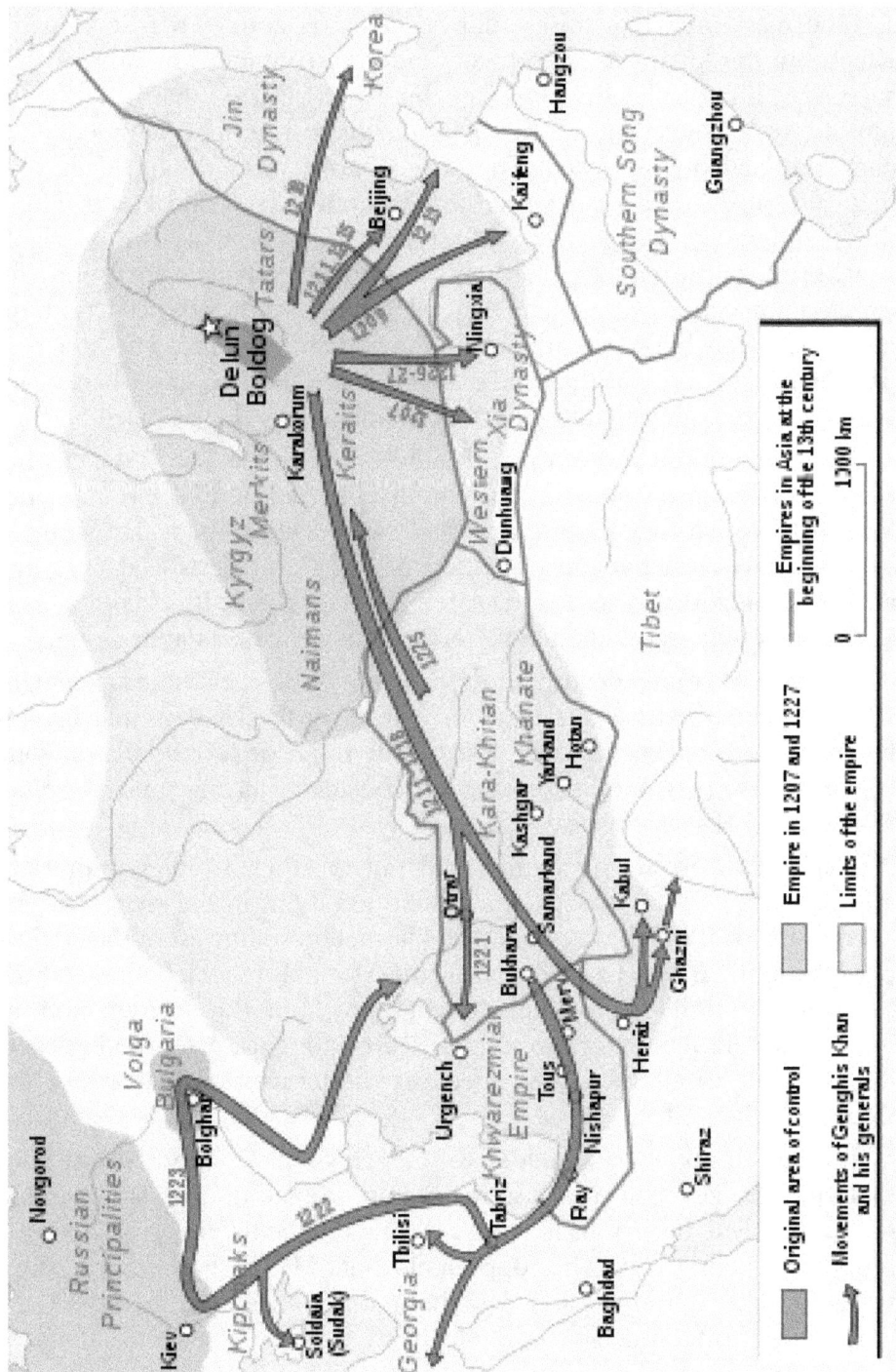

The campaigns of Genghis Khan from 1207 to 1225. [10]

One may think that this would be taken as good news by Genghis Khan, but the khan was already looking toward Sultan Muhammad II's successor, his son, Jalal al-Din. Genghis Khan realized that in order for him to truly lay claim to the Khwarazmian Empire, he needed to eliminate Jalal al-Din as well. The Mongol army was led into Persia, and they laid siege to great cities such as Nishapur, Merv, and Herat. Here, the people were slaughtered with relative abandon, as the Mongols sought to instill fear and terror into the populace. This is apparently no exaggeration since Mongolian general Subutai directed his troops to indiscriminately kill all the men, women, and children they encountered. The killing was so bad that, in some instances, certain cities had death tolls that were higher than the normal population of the city itself.

How is that possible? People who did not normally live in the city but rather dwelled in the surrounding countryside had poured into the cities for refuge. What they found, however, was a death trap, as the Mongols stormed into even the most fortified of cities and destroyed everyone and everything (even cats weren't safe!) inside of them. It is said that over a million people were killed in the once great city of Nishapur alone.

So, why all of this death and destruction? The ever-ruthless Genghis Khan wanted to demonstrate to the citizenry that he was playing for keeps. He wanted to basically destroy any hope or morale that anyone had so that they would not even consider rallying under Sultan Muhammad II's successor.

Jalal al-Din, in the meantime, had put together a rather impressive army of some 60,000 troops and positioned them in the vicinity of the town of Ghazni, which was some 150 kilometers southwest of the Afghan city of Kabul. He was basically daring the Mongols to attack him, and the Mongols took the bait. They fought hard, but the fortress and its defenders were ultimately too much for the Mongols. After the besiegers lost over one thousand troops needlessly trying to take the fortress, the siege was called off.

It then fell upon the shoulders of Genghis Khan's adopted son Shigi Qutuqu, who also had troops in the region, to pick up the slack. He did not want to lose his troops to such a formidable target either, so he came up with a plan to lure his opponents out. He created several straw scarecrow-like dummies and put them on horses. He then sent the "straw army" off to one side of the fortress.

The trick worked. Jalal al-Din actually thought it was a real army. The sighting spooked some of Jalal al-Din's officers enough into recommending a retreat. Jalal al-Din was not spooked that easily, though. He insisted that they stand and fight. He was lucky to trust his own judgment on this, for if they had exited the fortress, the real army would have come down on them in all directions. Shigi Qutuqu's men tried to lay siege to the fortress once again, only to be repulsed and sustain severe losses.

However, Jalal al-Din was having problems of his own. Some of his Turkish mercenaries revolted against him. As chaos erupted, Jalal al-Din quickly withdrew with what remained of his loyal troops and crossed the Indus River before making his way to what we now call Pakistan.

Shortly thereafter, Jalal al-Din was made aware that a resurgent Mongolian force had picked up his trail and was giving chase. He was eventually cornered. If his loyal bodyguards had not been there, he would have been killed. The guards stood between him and the Mongols until nearly all of them were destroyed.

At the last possible moment, Jalal al-Din managed to jump into the water below and swim to safety. He was able to find refuge within the domain of the sultan of Delhi.

He had escaped, but just like his father, he died shortly thereafter. Jalal al-Din was apparently killed by a local who accused him of banditry. With one great leader perishing of pneumonia and another killed as if he were nothing more than a common bandit, the end of the Khwarazmian Empire had arrived. The Mongols were now the undisputed leaders of a huge swathe of land that stretched from China to Iran.

By this point, Genghis Khan had set in motion an empire-building machine, although he was not always at the forefront of it. The empire rapidly expanded in all directions, and many of these conquests were led by either his sons or his top generals. One such general was named Jebe. This most trusted of Genghis Khan's generals actually first encountered the great khan as an opponent.

Back then, he was not known as Jebe. He was known by another name, Zurgadai. Young Zurgadai had been defending his homeland from a Mongol incursion when, somehow or other, he managed to get Genghis Khan in his sights. He fired an arrow from a great distance with such force and accuracy that it seemed to defy odds and connect to its target. The arrow lodged in Genghis Khan's neck.

Although the injury was not fatal, it was enough to startle Genghis Khan. He was not going to simply forget about it either. As soon as his army was victorious over the combatants, the first thing he wanted to know was who had fired the arrow that had hit him in the neck. Zurgadai could have kept quiet, but it was not in his nature to shirk or shy away from confrontation. He readily admitted to being the one who had fired off the arrow. He then declared that he was willing to pay the ultimate price and be executed for his actions. However, if the khan should decide to spare his life, he pledged that he would be his most loyal warrior.

Genghis Khan seemed to have been intrigued by both the audacity and the honesty of this man and agreed to his terms. From that day forward, Zurgadai was known as Jebe, which means "arrow," and he went on to become one of Genghis Khan's best generals.

Jebe would lead the charge into eastern Europe, where he laid the groundwork for a long-lasting khanate that would become known as the Golden Horde. Aiding him in this was Genghis Khan's other trusted general, Subutai.

Subutai also has an interesting backstory, like Jebe. He was said to have been an impoverished nomad who was able to rise up in the ranks because of his outstanding service. His example is often pointed to as evidence that Genghis Khan's army valued meritocracy. In other words, Genghis Khan was more interested in those who had the right skills for the job than in their birth.

Subutai was indeed known as a relentlessly hard worker. It has been said that shortly after the fall of the Khwarazmian Empire, Genghis Khan asked Subutai to report to him from where he was in Samarkand. This was quite a distance to cover, but Subutai, determined to get there as soon as possible, hopped on a fast horse and rode off as quickly as those four feet could take him.

During this trek, he actually tied himself to the horse so that he could sleep while riding if necessary. This practically non-stop journey allowed him to cover over one thousand miles in a week, which was an incredible thing to do on horseback.

In the aftermath of the conquest of the Khwarazmian Empire, Subutai hooked up with Jebe, and the two began to push even farther west. They did this after asking the great khan's permission, of course. Genghis Khan was likely relieved to be able to take a break and have two of his most competent generals fighting on his behalf. He readily agreed to the arrangement.

This started the great Mongol push into eastern Europe. First, they sent around twenty thousand warriors into Azerbaijan. Here, they took down several cities, although they spared the city of Tabriz. This was only due to a special gift made by the emperor of Azerbaijan. His gift came in the form of money, clothes, and horses, which managed to bribe the Mongols enough to forego another siege.

Jebe and Subutai were essentially able to take a break after this and had something like a mini-vacation in the warm and welcoming city of Tabriz as they planned their next major military campaign. Their next major assault would be aimed at the eastern European country of Georgia.

Georgia is an ancient land with a long and proud history, rooted in the Eastern Orthodox Christian faith. To the Georgians, the arrival of the Mongols must have seemed like a scourge from hell itself. The Mongols came not only with steel and fire but with a weapon just as terrifying—fear. Wherever they went, they made sure that tales of their cruelty spread faster than their armies. Towns that resisted were obliterated, survivors were paraded as examples, and the psychological weight of their advance often crushed their enemies long before swords ever clashed.

When the Mongols descended upon Georgia in 1220, they brought this strategy with them. Their army stretched as far as the eye could see. Yet, King George IV of Georgia, known as Lasha George, did not flinch. He rallied his nobles and troops, determined to defend his kingdom against the onslaught.

At first, the Georgians seemed to have some success. Their cavalry smashed into the Mongol vanguard and inflicted heavy losses, forcing a temporary retreat. For a brief moment, hope flickered that perhaps the Mongols could be driven back. However, this was precisely the kind of trap the Mongols had perfected.

When the Georgians pressed forward, the true scale of the Mongol army revealed itself. Subutai and Jebe unleashed their full might, with disciplined horse archers surrounding the Georgian forces on multiple sides. Showers of arrows rained down, breaking cohesion and sowing panic. What had looked like a chance at victory dissolved into catastrophe. Thousands of Georgians fell where they stood. King George himself was gravely wounded in the fighting, an injury from which he would never recover. He died a few years later from his wound.

The Georgian stand had been valiant, but it was crushed beneath the same blend of cunning and brutality that had already toppled so many others. The Mongols stormed through Georgia and made it their own. More conquests followed in quick succession in the borderlands between Azerbaijan and modern-day Iran. Armenia also fell in a similar fashion.

Armenia was the first country to officially adopt Christianity as its state religion, and those of this land of deep faith were deeply perplexed. It was hard for them to countenance the fact that they had been overrun by a bunch of godless nomads in such a brutal fashion. They fell into a common trap that many Christians might fall into. They blamed God for the unfortunate events that occurred in a world full of free will. People make their own choices (many of them being bad ones) every single step of the way. The Armenians had to learn that, despite their deep faith, they did not live in heaven but rather in a fallen world. They had to deal with the nature of that fallen state. If they were going to resist what had been foisted upon them, it was up to them to do it.

The Mongols, relentless in their push westward, soon reached the forbidding wall of the Caucasus Mountains. Here, the journey itself became as dangerous as any foe. The high passes were full of snow and bitter winds. Many men froze in the saddle, while others fell victim to sickness in the harsh, thin air. Contemporary accounts say that hundreds died from frostbite and exposure before the army ever saw an enemy's blade. Yet, even in such a place, the Mongols found ways to survive. Some mountain peoples weighed their chances and struck bargains with Subutai and Jebe. In exchange for sparing their villages, they offered guides to lead the horsemen through treacherous paths. With this local knowledge at their side, the Mongols made their way through the Caucasus and descended at last into the lands beyond.

But here they found no peace. On the other side of the mountains lay the Alans and their allies, warriors who fought in ways the Mongols recognized all too well. They used ambushes, swift attacks, and sudden retreats. The clashes with the Alans dragged on, and they were brutal and costly. To break the stalemate, the Mongols turned to their gift for diplomacy and deception. They approached the Cumans, old enemies of the Alans, and promised them an alliance. United, the Mongols and

Cumans struck at the Alan defenses with overwhelming force. The Alans were crushed.

Yet the Cumans soon discovered what countless others would learn. Mongol friendship seldom lasted long. With the Alans destroyed, the Mongols turned on their former allies. Cuman bands were hunted down, their herds were seized, and their families were scattered. The betrayal was swift and merciless.

From there, the Mongols drove deeper into the Black Sea steppe. Their campaign spilled into Crimea, where rich trading colonies dotted the coast. Among them was the Genoese stronghold of Sudak, or Soldaia. The merchants of Genoa had grown wealthy off the commerce of the region, but their stone walls and bustling markets offered no shield against the storm of Mongol arrows. Sudak was sacked and left in ruins.

The raid into Crimea alarmed the princes of Rus', as well as the surviving Cumans, who had fled north to seek protection. They carried with them tales of fire and slaughter and pleaded for aid. The Rus', though divided by rivalries, could not ignore such a threat pressing so close to their borders. Reluctantly, they began to muster their forces. The stage was set for a confrontation unlike any they had ever faced. The Mongols, fresh from their triumphs in the Caucasus and Crimea, turned their attention to the heartlands of Kievan Rus'.

In 1223, a coalition army of Rus' princes, joined by their Cuman allies, confronted Subutai and Jebe on the steppe. Although the Mongols were bold, they did not march blindly into the coalition's full strength. Instead, they employed one of their most trusted strategies: the feigned retreat. The clash began with skirmishes and quick assaults by mounted archers who loosed arrows and then wheeled away. To the Rus', it looked as if the Mongols were faltering. Their horsemen seemed to melt into the horizon, as though abandoning the field altogether.

Believing the enemy to be in flight, the Rus' princes grew confident. Over several days, they pressed the Mongols across the steppe. The chase stretched on, long enough to exhaust their men and thin their lines. The Cumans urged their horses on, convinced that the Mongols were on the run, and the princes, eager for glory, listened. The coalition army stretched ever farther, which meant cohesion began to slip away. It was exactly what Subutai wanted.

At last, near the banks of the Kalka River, the Mongols turned. They had chosen their ground carefully. Behind them lay slopes and open plains; it was perfect for cavalry maneuvers. As the weary Rus' forces approached, Subutai unleashed his heavy horsemen in a sudden and crushing charge. What seemed a panicked flight became a whirlwind counterattack. Arrows darkened the sky, hooves thundered, and the stretched lines of the Rus' army buckled.

The rout was merciless. Thousands were cut down in place. Others fled in terror, only to be trampled or drowned in the crossing. The princes fought with desperate valor, but their courage alone could not withstand the Mongol tactics. Soon, the battlefield was strewn with corpses.

Prince Mstislav of Galicia escaped by boat down the Dnieper. His army was ruined, but he was still alive. Mstislav Romanovich, Prince of Kiev, was not so fortunate. Captured with other nobles, he suffered a death that seared itself into the memory of the Rus'. The Mongols laid planks across their bodies and then feasted atop them. As the victors drank and sang, the weight bore down until the princes suffocated beneath the boards.

When the slaughter was done, the Mongols did not remain to hold the land. This had been a reconnaissance mission, not a conquest. Subutai and Jebe withdrew eastward. The march home was grueling. Jebe would not survive the journey. He died along the way, likely from illness. Subutai returned to Mongolia with priceless knowledge of the western steppe. He would rise further in the ranks, becoming one of Genghis Khan's greatest commanders and, in time, leading campaigns that carved scars into Europe.

The Battle of the Kalka River revealed that the Mongols were no passing storm but a force capable of smashing armies many times their size. It also showed that disunity among the Rus' was fatal. Only a united front could stand a chance against the Mongols. Genghis Khan would not live long after these events, dying in 1227, but the lessons of the Battle of the Kalka River returned east with his generals. His heirs would remember them well.

Chapter 7: Genghis Khan and His Immediate Successors

"What a pity that the superhuman glory of his century—Genghis Khan—bent his bow and took aim only at eagles!"

-Mao Zedong[1]

By the summer of 1222, Genghis Khan was no longer the young warrior who had clawed his way up from obscurity. Now in his early sixties—quite an old age to reach on the harsh steppes—he could feel time catching up with him. Though still vigorous, he knew his body bore the weight of years spent in the saddle, of campaigns fought across half the world. He began to wonder whether even the greatest of conquerors could hold back the shadow that stalks all men.

As he toured his newly won territories, he welcomed not only envoys and bearers of tribute but also philosophers and holy men. They came from many traditions—Buddhist, Muslim, Christian, and Daoist—and all were allowed to speak. Some talked about hidden secrets, elixirs, and potions that could prolong one's life. For Genghis Khan, who cared little for speculation about the afterlife, this was the subject that truly gripped him. He wanted to know if he could live even longer, perhaps forever.

Among those who came to his camp was the Daoist master Qiu Chuji, also known as Master Changchun, "Everlasting Spring." Rumors claimed he was more than a century old. If anyone held the secret of

---

[1] Hoang, Michel. *Genghis Khan.* 1988. Pg. 285.

immortality, he surely would. Intrigued, Genghis sent for him. In 1222, the sage finally arrived at the khan's encampment in Central Asia.

Genghis greeted him with the question that lay heavy on his mind: was there truly an elixir of eternal life? Could the ravages of age be turned aside by hidden knowledge?

Qiu Chuji did not flatter Genghis Khan, and he did not bend the truth. He told the khan that no potion could cheat death. The dream of immortality was an illusion. However, he offered another kind of counsel. The surest path to a long life, he said, was not magic but temperance—to avoid excess, to rule with justice, to show mercy, and to live in balance with the world.

To Genghis Khan, who had been promised many things by many men, this blunt honesty was a revelation. He respected Qiu Chuji's candor and rewarded him accordingly. The sage's followers were granted privileges and exemptions, and the khan kept him close as an advisor.

The year 1223 was one of great expansion for the potential successors of Genghis Khan. Although the great khan was still alive, it was as if all of the potential inheritors of his empire were scrambling to outdo each other and show just who had the greatest fire in their belly as it pertained to taking over for Genghis Khan after he was gone.

As his subordinates were making tremendous inroads of conquest and territorial gain, Genghis Khan himself was coming to grips with his own mortality. No matter how much his sons and generals conquered and no matter how many armies they defeated, he knew that he was just one mortal man and that his own time on Earth was rapidly drawing to a close.

In 1224, with the western campaigns concluded and the Khwarazmian Empire shattered, Genghis Khan returned to Mongolia. For the first time in years, he was not actively on campaign, and he used this brief respite to consolidate his rule. The steppe nobles gathered to celebrate their victories, and for a while, the khan allowed himself the rare luxury of resting. During this period of reflection, he began to think more earnestly about succession and how to preserve unity once he was gone.

Genghis Khan determined that the great holdings he had conquered should be divided up into separate khanates, which were similar to kingdoms, that would be allocated to his sons. He gave the distinction of supreme khan to Ogedei, while the other sons ruled their various realms essentially as governors.

However, his rest did not last long. In 1225, reports arrived from the western fringes of his empire. Trouble was brewing in the Tangut kingdom of Western Xia. This was the very state that had first recognized his authority two decades earlier, but now they were beginning to defy him by withholding tribute and forming alliances with his enemies. For Genghis Khan, who valued loyalty above all else, this betrayal was intolerable.

By 1226, Genghis Khan was once again on the move. Though in his sixties, he mounted up to personally lead a massive campaign against the Tangut kingdom. He was determined to punish them once and for all for breaking their oaths of loyalty. The Mongol army that gathered was enormous, numbering well over 100,000 hardened riders who were fresh from victories in China and Central Asia.

The Tanguts were not in a position to resist. Their kingdom had already been weakened by decades of paying Mongol tribute, and they had no allies willing to come to their aid. The Jin dynasty was on the verge of total collapse, and the Song dynasty had no interest in intervening. When the Mongols crossed their borders, they met only scattered resistance.

Town after town fell. The Mongols struck first at frontier fortresses and trading hubs, cutting off supply lines and making it impossible for the Tanguts to regroup. Villages that resisted were wiped out. Those that surrendered were often spared, but they were still stripped of their wealth to remind them of the Mongols' supremacy.

One of the early targets was the stronghold of Khara-Khoto on the edge of the desert. Its fall opened the way deeper into the Tangut lands. From there, the Mongols fanned out across the countryside, burning fields, scattering armies, and leaving no safe refuge. The Tangut emperor, Li Xian, tried to rally his people, but morale collapsed quickly in the face of such relentless devastation.

By the end of 1226, the Mongols had reduced much of Western Xia to ruins. For Genghis Khan, this was not another raid to enforce tribute; it was a campaign of extermination. The Tanguts had defied him, and he meant to erase them from the map.

By early 1227, the Mongols had driven the Tanguts back to their capital at Zhongxing. The city was swollen with refugees, and its supplies were running dangerously low. The emperor sent desperate appeals for peace, but Genghis Khan was not interested. He had already decided that Western Xia would cease to exist.

The siege dragged on for months. Mongol engineers built siege towers and catapults, hurling stones and fire into the city. They cut off all routes of escape, waiting patiently as hunger and disease gnawed away at the defenders inside. The emperor's pleas grew more frantic, but Genghis Khan refused to negotiate.

It was during this final campaign that Genghis Khan himself fell ill. Some later accounts claimed he was thrown from his horse, while others say that he was stricken with fever or even wounded in battle. There is even an account that says he was struck by lightning. Whatever the cause, his health began to fail in the summer of 1227. Still, he pressed on, unwilling to show weakness to his enemies or even to his own men.

In August, as Zhongxing prepared to surrender, Genghis Khan died. His generals and sons immediately swore to keep his death a secret until the campaign was finished. The Mongol army stormed the city, sacking it completely and reducing it to rubble.

The details of his burial remain one of history's mysteries. Tradition holds that he was carried back to Mongolia and interred in an unmarked grave somewhere near the sacred Burkhan Khaldun (a mountain in northeastern Mongolia). Those who attended the funeral are said to have been killed to preserve the secret. Whatever the truth, his death marked the end of an era.

Genghis Khan's passing meant that the title of universal ruler, or khagan, would fall to his chosen heir—his third son, Ogedei. Unlike his stern and iron-willed father, Ogedei was remembered as a genial, generous man who enjoyed life's pleasures to excess. He was a proven commander in war, but he had also earned a reputation as a lover of drink and merriment, with feasts and revelry ranking high among his priorities. Now, however, the mantle of supreme leadership rested upon his shoulders, and the future of the empire depended upon him.

A portrait of Ogedei.[11]

Outside of the innermost circle, few even knew that such a transfer of power had taken place. Immediately after Genghis Khan's death in 1227, his commanders worked feverishly to conceal the truth. They feared that any premature announcement might spark claims to the throne before Ogedei's succession could be formally secured.

So carefully was the news guarded that later generations told chilling tales of the funeral guard killing any wayward traveler who stumbled across the great khan's procession, lest the secret escape. Whether or not this grim story was actually true, it shows the lengths to which the Mongols went to preserve silence around their leader's passing. To the outside world, the thunder of Mongol hooves continued as if nothing had changed. Only when Ogedei was enthroned did the truth finally emerge. The man who had reshaped Eurasia was gone, and a new chapter of conquest was about to begin.

Ogedei also had to keep in mind that it was all of the newly conquered vassal states paying tribute that allowed him to have such a lavish and extravagant lifestyle. When he took power, he was determined to show that the empire could not only conquer but also endure. In 1230, he launched a major campaign against the Jin dynasty in northern China, personally leading Mongol armies into the field. These victories brought immense wealth into the empire, and Ogedei quickly turned his attention to something his father had never done—constructing a true capital.

In 1235, he chose the city of Karakorum, a settlement in the Orkhon Valley, to serve as the empire's heart. On the broad Mongolian steppe, he ordered the building of a magnificent palace that would be large enough to house lavish banquets. There would also be administrative offices, marketplaces, and temples for many faiths. For a people who had long lived from their saddles, it was a startling transformation. Yet, Ogedei did not stop at one residence. Between 1235 and 1238, he ordered additional palaces built across Central Asia, ensuring that wherever he traveled, the khan could dwell in luxury.

At the same time, Mongol armies were spreading in every direction. In the east, Ogedei ordered the first great push against the Southern Song dynasty in 1235, though the campaigns met stiff resistance and failed to break through China's southern defenses. By 1239, the Mongols raided deep into Sichuan but were forced to withdraw. In the west, Mongol riders under Ogedei's nephews thundered into Europe. By the early 1240s, they had reached Budapest and Vienna, shocking Christendom with the scale of their advance.

In Poland, a coalition of knights and princes rode out to meet them, only to be utterly crushed at the Battle of Legnica in April 1241. Even the famed heavy cavalry of Europe proved no match for Mongol tactics.

Meanwhile, in Hungary, King Bela IV mustered his forces for what he hoped would be a decisive stand. The clash came on the Sajo River at the Battle of Mohi. It was one of the most catastrophic defeats in medieval history. The Hungarian army was annihilated, and the Mongol cavalry fanned out across the countryside, burning villages, destroying crops, and turning the kingdom into a wasteland. Refugees fled westward in terror, carrying tales of devastation that spread panic across Europe.

By the end of that year, Mongol forces had reached as far as Budapest and Vienna, standing at the threshold of western Christendom itself. To many, it seemed only a matter of time before France, Germany, and even Rome fell to the horsemen of the steppe. Chroniclers wrote in near-apocalyptic tones, convinced the end of the world was at hand.

Then, as suddenly as they had arrived, the Mongols turned back. The reason was not a defeat on the battlefield but news from the east. The Great Khan Ogedei had died in December 1241. Following tradition, the princes of the empire were required to return to Mongolia for a kurultai to decide the next ruler. Batu and Subutai reluctantly withdrew from the borders of Austria in 1242. Europe had been spared, though not by its own strength. It was sheer chance.

But before Ogedei died, he made sure that Karakorum grew into a true capital. Along with palaces, Ogedei ordered defensive walls to be raised around the city. The same people who had once prided themselves on tearing down the walls of others were now determined to guard their own. The Mongol Empire was changing. The steppe warriors were still fearsome, but they were becoming rulers of cities, administrators of trade, and masters of an empire that spanned continents.

One of the interesting things about Karakorum was just how dependent it was on outside trade. The steppes surrounding the city were not good for farming, so all of the city's food supply inevitably came from outside the city. This meant that the surrounding trade routes, especially the Silk Road trade routes, were of extreme importance. Ogedei saw to it that the roads were made secure by way of force.

The Mongols were doing well as far as trade was concerned, but as early as 1235, the revenue was just not stretching far enough. As such, the pressure began to mount among the Mongols to expand their territory since the number one driver of their prosperity in the past had always been plunder through conquest. The Mongols just had to figure out who would be in their crosshairs next.

To decide the next direction of conquest, Ogedei convened a kurultai, where his leading generals debated the future of the empire. Subutai, the brilliant strategist who had already carved his name into history on his campaigns from China to the Caucasus, urged the Mongols to strike farther west. His advice was taken, and in 1236, the armies under Batu Khan and Subutai swept into the Middle Volga, crushing the Volga Bulgars and clearing the way into the Rus' lands.

The storm broke first upon Ryazan in December 1237. The Mongols demanded the city's surrender, but the Rus' princes refused. The siege that followed was brutal. Mongol catapults and fire weapons battered the defenses, while cavalry patrols cut off all hope of escape. After only five days, Ryazan's walls were breached, and the city was put to the sword. Chronicles describe near-total destruction. Few inhabitants survived.

From there, the Mongols advanced relentlessly. Suzdal, Vladimir, and Moscow all fell in turn. Finally, in December 1240, they came to Kiev (modern-day Kyiv), the jewel of the Kievan Rus'. The defenders killed a Mongol envoy rather than surrender, which sealed their fate. The Mongols encircled the city, brought up massive siege engines, and hurled fire and stones until the walls crumbled. On December 6th, 1240, Kiev fell. Chronicles tell of streets choked with corpses and churches reduced to ash. The once-great capital was left in ruins.

Not every Rus' prince perished. Danylo of Halych, a survivor from the west, later traveled to the Mongol court at Sarai. There, to secure his rule, he swore allegiance to Batu Khan and performed the ritual of drinking fermented mare's milk—kumis—from the khan's own cup. It was a moment that symbolized the new order. The Rus' princes now served at the pleasure of the Mongols.

This domination was later known as the rule of the Golden Horde, and it would endure for more than two centuries. Only in the late 15th century would Moscow finally throw off the Mongol yoke. By then, the Golden Horde had long since fractured into rival khanates, fighting each other as often as their old enemies.

This was long past Ogedei's time, but this great khan would not even live to see the full establishment of the Golden Horde. Consumed with alcoholism and a wild, hedonistic life, he passed away in 1241.

There are some anecdotes about his final days. It has been said that he regularly suffered from tremors, but his faithful holy men attributed these not to alcoholic withdrawal symptoms but to demonic attacks! His court physicians declared that he had been cursed and was being routinely beset by evil spirits. They also had an interesting solution for all of this. They decided that the only way to free Ogedei from these bad spirits was to cast them out of Ogedei and into the body of a willing participant. Ogedei was battling his inner demons, and according to these shamans, he just needed to swap his demons with someone else's.

Interestingly, Ogedei's own brother, Tolui, stepped up as a volunteer and agreed to take on his brother's evil spirits. Even though it would pain him to do so, he reasoned that his brother's life was more important than his and that the whole realm would benefit if he were healed and of sound mind.

It is unclear exactly how the ritual of demon transference went down. It apparently involved Tolui consuming a large amount of alcohol himself, filling himself with the same familiar spirits as his brother Ogedei so often drank. According to legend, he drank so much in one sitting that he actually died.[i]

It is difficult to think how such a thing could have helped Ogedei, but for people utterly consumed by superstitious thinking, anything seemed possible. Whatever they might have thought about it, Ogedei died not long after his brother's valiant sacrifice.

In the meantime, the Mongol forces had pushed farther and farther into eastern Europe until their empire stretched from the Mongolian steppes to clear across the whole Eurasian Steppe. These inroads were made under Jochi and then furthered by Jochi's son, Batu.

In truth, Jochi never entirely escaped the shadow of doubt. Born after Borte's capture by the Merkit, whispers about his paternity dogged him all his life. Though Genghis recognized him as his son, their relationship soured in later years. Jochi preferred ruling the rich western steppes he had subdued, while his father demanded unrelenting conquest. Their quarrel grew so bad that Jochi refused to answer Genghis's summons. Rumors spread that the great khan was prepared to march against his own son. Fate intervened first. Jochi died in early 1227, only months before Genghis himself. Jochi left his inheritance to his son, Batu.

Although his name is somewhat forgotten in the historic telling of the Mongol Empire, overshadowed by names such as Subutai, Ogedei, Kublai Khan, and, of course, the great Genghis Khan himself, Batu was indeed a major force in the push across the steppes and especially in the establishment of what came to be known as the Golden Horde.

In the aftermath of Ogedei's death in 1241, Batu and his forces found themselves pushing up the Volga River. They ended up setting up their camp in the vicinity of Atil, which had once served as the capital of the

---

[i] Clements, Jonathan. *A Brief History of Khubilai Khan: Lord of Xanadu, Emperor of China.* 2010. Pg. 23.

Khazars. The Khazars, who also originally hailed from the steppes, were Turkic in origin and had set up shop on the Volga during the 6th century.

The Khazars and their brief but flourishing civilization represent a unique moment in history. During a time of intense religious ideology, especially as it pertained to the struggles between Christianity and Islam, the Khazars became the only known nation (outside of perhaps ancient Israel) to adopt Judaism as their official religion. The Khazars were initially quite prosperous, relying primarily on trade. They established a valuable trading hub in the region. In fact, they were great partners for a time with the Byzantine Empire, both as it pertained to commercial trade and as a potential military ally.

However, not everyone appreciated the Khazars. In the 10th century, the Kievan Rus', the founding tribe of what would become both Ukraine and Russia, descended on them in force. The Kievan Rus' were able to overcome the Khazars and utterly destroy their civilization. It was right on top of these noble ruins that the Mongols, led by the wily Batu, had found themselves.

After the Mongols pushed through the steppes and passed into Eurasia, they pushed even farther into Europe, reaching Albania. They were prepared to march all the way to Vienna. However, when Batu heard of Ogedei's death in 1241, these plans were called off. This was due to the fact that it was Mongol custom for all of the princely heirs to Genghis Khan (Batu included) to be in attendance for the kurultai to decide who would be Ogedei's successor. The council members needed to choose who would take the role of universal leader.

After Ogedei's passing, his wife, Toregene, briefly took over as the head of the Mongol Empire. There was no official recognition of her as empress or anything of that nature, but she was the one who wielded power after her husband's passing.

Initially, efforts were made to make her oldest son, Guyuk, the new khan. However, this went against Ogedei's own wishes since he had intimated before his passing that he felt that Guyuk's temperament was simply not right for the job. Guyuk was apparently prone to having a bad temper, so he would not be the best ruler when it came to making administrative decisions.

Instead of Guyuk, Ogedei preferred for his successor to be his grandson and Guyuk's own nephew, Shiremun.[i] Toregene was determined to defy Ogedei's wishes. She wanted Guyuk to succeed regardless of how her late husband had felt. In August of 1246, Guyuk was officially granted the status of khan.

Toregene had followed her own ambition, but she would come to regret it. Guyuk lived up to all of his father's fears about him being too temperamental to govern. The first sign of trouble came when he turned against the officials his mother had appointed during her regency. He dismissed many of them outright. He especially hated one of Toregene's closest advisors, a Persian woman named Fatima. Fatima had wielded enormous influence under the regency, but once Guyuk secured power, she was accused of treachery and put to death.

One striking feature of the Mongol Empire was how often women served in the government. Female advisors, regents, and patrons were far more common among the Mongols than in most of their contemporaries. This was particularly true of women tied to the imperial family through blood, marriage, or friendship. Historians have long remarked that Mongol women played larger roles in society at every level. Marco Polo himself noted how Mongol women seemed to carry the weight of the household while their men rode to hunt or wage war. His account may oversimplify the situation, but it certainly seems that women were used to managing families, livestock, and trade in their husbands' absence.

These traditions carried into Mongol rule abroad. Women not only managed households but also held property, advised rulers, and sometimes even commanded in war. In China, the Mongols encountered the troubling custom of female infanticide, which was driven by their preference for sons. Some sources suggest that Mongol rulers attempted to discourage the practice, though it had little lasting effect. Even so, it is noteworthy that such concerns were raised at all in a world where the fate of infant girls was too often ignored.[ii]

Regardless of how much a female advisor such as Fatima might have been valued in the Mongol court, Guyuk was certainly not too fond of her. According to most accounts, he actually claimed the woman was a

---

[i] Clements, Jonathan. *A Brief History of Khubilai Khan: Lord of Xanadu, Emperor of China.* 2010. Pg. 27.

[ii] Fitzhugh, William. *Genghis Khan and the Mongol Empire.* 2009. Pg. 110.

witch and demanded that she be thrown in prison. Today, these kinds of claims rightfully sound outrageous. But could there have been something other than witchcraft that irked Guyuk? According to some sources, Fatima had been quite busy during her stint as an unofficial cabinet official (the Mongols never had an official cabinet, but they had an informal system that very much mimicked it). In particular, she saw to it that northern China was heavily taxed, the proceeds of which she turned over to Toregene.

Such things made the citizenry of northern China understandably restless. They were so restless that open revolt was likely not out of the question. Could it be that Guyuk's more practical reason to depose Fatima was to put an end to all of these overreaching tax hikes? Could he have feared an open revolt if he did not put a stop to Fatima's antics and alleviate some of the burden she had created?

Whatever the case might have been, Fatima was initially out of Guyuk's reach since his mother protected her with her own bodyguards. This created a kind of stand-off between Guyuk's guards and his mother's guards.

Eventually, Guyuk's guards prevailed, and they managed to seize Fatima. It is not clear exactly what happened, but Guyuk's own mother was killed in the process. Guyuk then took out his rage on poor Fatima. She was savagely tortured. Guyuk then placed her battered body on display for all to see.

Fortunately for the Mongolians and anyone else concerned about what was going on in the empire, Guyuk's reign of terror was short, and he abruptly passed away in 1248. He was forty-two years old at the time, and it is believed that he either succumbed to alcoholism or was poisoned.

Interestingly, in that same fateful year of 1248, one of Genghis Khan's most trusted generals, Subutai, passed away. With the death of so many notable figures in the empire—Guyuk Khan, Subutai, and others—many who had pledged allegiance to the Mongol horde began to quietly test its armor for weak points. From Europe to the Middle East, subject rulers wondered whether the empire might finally be vulnerable.

One such figure was the Kievan Rus' prince Danylo of Halych. Years earlier, he had bent the knee to Batu Khan, even submitting to the ritual of drinking fermented mare's milk. That bitter draft sealed his loyalty, but in time, it soured. By the early 1250s, as the Mongol court fractured in the wake of succession disputes, Danylo began to see a chance to break free.

In 1253, he appealed to Pope Innocent IV and to Hungary and other European kingdoms, urging them to mount a crusade against the Mongols. The plan sounded bold on paper—a Christian coalition to liberate the Rus' from foreign domination—but it never materialized. Europe was too divided and too hesitant to face the Mongols directly. Danylo pressed ahead on his own, though, seizing Podolia and parts of Volhynia. He hoped to strengthen his hand while the Mongols were distracted.

For a brief moment, it seemed as though he had succeeded. The Mongols were preoccupied with infighting, so they ignored his defiance. However, by the mid-1250s, they returned. Batu Khan's successors summoned Danylo to account for his actions. Ever the survivor, he shifted his stance once more. Realizing that his European allies had abandoned him, he made peace with the Mongols, reaffirming his loyalty in person at Sarai, their capital on the Volga. According to later accounts, he again partook in the ritual of drinking kumis, a symbolic gesture that bound him to the horde.

The Mongols demanded more than words this time. They called on Danylo to aid their campaigns in Poland and Lithuania. Though these expeditions were eventually beaten back, the Mongols maintained their iron grip over Rus' lands. For the next two centuries, their overlordship shaped the destiny of the region.

Before the Mongol invasion, Kiev had been the great power of the steppe world, as it was a flourishing center of trade and culture. But the devastation of 1240 shattered its dominance. In the vacuum, another city rose—Moscow. Over time, Moscow would eclipse Kiev as the beating heart of the Russian world. This shift, caused in no small part by Mongol conquest and policy, would echo for centuries.

It was a tumultuous, dynamic age for the empire of Genghis Khan. Each region took on a life of its own, shaped by the ambitions of local rulers and the decisions of khans in Karakorum and Sarai. Guyuk's passing had opened a new succession crisis, and yet, out of this turbulence, another towering leader would soon emerge, one whose name would rival even that of Genghis himself. He was none other than Kublai Khan.

Chapter 8: The Rise of Kublai Khan

"With whom lie the advantages derived from Heaven and Earth? On which side is discipline most rigorously enforced? Which army is stronger? On which side are officers and men more highly trained? In which army is there the greater constancy both in reward and punishment?"

-Sun Tzu[1]

In the aftermath of Guyuk's passing, there were, predictably enough, several claimants to the Mongolian throne. The empire had been broken up into several khanates with their own respective khan, or governor, but all of these rulers were supposed to still be under the control of the great universal ruler.

The closest claimant for this title by familial lines was Guyuk's cousin, Mongke. This new claimant was actually the son of the ill-fated Tolui, the brother of Ogedei, who died attempting to absorb the spirits that had plagued Ogedei. Mongke was definitely in the line of succession, but there was still the question of Shiremun, who had actually been Ogedei's choice for successor in the first place.

Shiremun was eager to stake his claim, and he was willing to do so by force if necessary. He actually assembled an army and began to march

---

[1] Sverdrup, Carl. *The Mongol Conquests: The Military Operations of Genghis Khan and Sube'etei.* 2017. Pg. 452.

toward Mongke's encampment. On the way there, however, a wagon that was part of his train ended up with a busted wagon wheel. This meant that necessary repairs had to be made.

Shiremun decided that he was not going to stick around for that. Instead, he had the bulk of his army continue with him, while those who stayed behind continued their duties repairing the wagon. However, after Shiremun departed, those tasked with this repair work were visited by a group of passing Mongols who desired to help. As they were aiding Shiremun's men, the disgruntled repairmen apparently blurted out the whole reason for their trip.

The kind Mongol strangers who helped the crew took quiet note of all of this and immediately reported all they had seen and heard back to Mongke himself. Mongke was then able to confront Shiremun with what he had learned. This obviously threw a wrench in Shiremun's plans, but he was quick to make up stories. He claimed that the huge entourage he was traveling with was merely on its way to show its respects. Mongke did not believe it.

Instead of simply cutting him down where he stood, Mongke had Shiremun arrested and brought before him. The plot was laid bare. Shiremun confessed to his bid for power and even admitted to rallying men to storm the kurultai. For a brief time, he sought protection under Kublai Khan, but when Mongke demanded his surrender, Kublai did not resist. To have sheltered a traitor any longer would have stained his own loyalty.

Shiremun was handed over and placed under judgment. This was no rash execution, though. Mongke wanted it clear to all the Mongol princes that he acted lawfully, not out of personal vengeance. Only after a formal reckoning was Shiremun condemned. He and many of his closest supporters were executed. Their deaths showed everyone that challenging the khan's authority would be met with harsh punishment.

Mongke was given the status of great khan for a short period. Despite his occasional heavy-handedness, he proved himself a good leader. He was of a wise and sound mind. Mongke kickstarted several great programs of development and revitalization for the empire. He also began to look at finishing the job of conquering the rest of China.

The Mongols had already toppled the Jurchen Jin dynasty, which had seized northern China from the Song dynasty in the early 12th century. Now, the Mongols turned their attention to the Southern Song dynasty, which had survived in the south for over a century. Their ultimate goal was the unification of all China under Mongol rule.

Interestingly, from the perspective of the Song dynasty, the situation—at least initially—did not seem all that different. They had fended off incursions from the Jin in the north for quite some time, and now they were faced with similar incursions, except these were being led by a different group of belligerents. For the Song dynasty, it seemed like it was just more of the same, but soon enough, they would learn that the Mongols were a worse threat than the Jin ever had been.

For a brief shining moment, Mongke was leading the charge. During the start of his push into Song territory, he was actually alarmed to learn that the Song had regained some of their previously lost ground.[i] The city of Xiangyang, for example, had been reclaimed by the Song and temporarily occupied by their garrisons.

In that sense, the Mongol offensive into Song China could, to some extent, be viewed as a kind of preemptive invasion. If the Mongols had not pushed deeper into Song territory, then a resurgent Song dynasty would have likely pushed deeper into what had already been claimed by the Mongols. For his part, Mongke was determined to prevent any such thing from happening.

Interestingly, the first major preparations he made during the build-up to war had less to do with martial might than environmental adaptation. The Mongols were born and raised in the cold steppes north of China. However, Mongke knew that the climate of southern China was a lot different.[ii] Southern China, by contrast, can be very hot and humid. In these kinds of conditions, disease and heat-induced exhaustion can run rampant. Mongke also knew that the Chinese had heavily fortified their cities in the south. This meant that the Mongols would be stuck outside of the cities for a long duration of time in the humid heat as they laid siege to these formidable cities.

Mongke started his push into China with fierce determination. It would not last for long, though, because Mongke himself was not long for this world. Just as the first offensives against the Song dynasty were underway, Mongke Khan abruptly perished of dysentery on August 11th,

[i] Clements, Jonathan. *A Brief History of Khubilai Khan: Lord of Xanadu, Emperor of China.* 2010. Pg. 41.
[ii] Clements, Jonathan. *A Brief History of Khubilai Khan: Lord of Xanadu, Emperor of China.* 2010. Pg. 62.

1259. Yes, at the age of fifty-one, he became a victim of the same sort of dreaded pestilence that the Mongols had been warned about.[i]

After his death, his younger brother Kublai Khan took over. Kublai Khan would truly revitalize the state of Mongolian warfare over the next several years. It was not always a smooth transition for Kublai Khan, as his leadership was occasionally challenged. For instance, Kublai Khan's younger brother, Ariq Boke, began to resist his leadership.

The crafty Ariq Boke appealed to more conservative elements, and he managed to get several high-ranking Mongols on his side. To these conservatives, Ariq Boke presented himself as a true Mongolian leader, and he disparaged his brother, Kublai Khan, for having picked up the habits of foreigners. He particularly disparaged his brother for having supposedly picked up the habits of the Chinese.[ii]

These arguments might seem rather superficial, but they must have struck a chord. Ariq Boke managed to kick off a kurultai in 1260, which had him declared the new khan. However, one has to consider who made up this council. More than likely, it was stacked with those who already supported Ariq Boke in the first place.

Kublai Khan did not let this bother him; he simply held a kurultai of his own and had his own supporters declare him khan all the same. There were now two clear claimants to the throne. If this matter were not resolved quickly, it would lead to an all-out civil war.

Seeking to deliver a knockout blow, Kublai Khan sent his forces straight for the designated capital of the empire, Karakorum. Those defending the great Mongolian capital tried their best to stave off the advancing army, but the odds were stacked against them. Not only did they face Kublai Khan's seasoned troops, but they also suffered from a deliberate and devastating cut-off of supplies. Karakorum was never intended to withstand a drawn-out siege, and it began to wither under the pressure. As hunger and hardship mounted, the people's will to resist began to crumble. Eventually, the city surrendered.

Even so, Ariq Boke was nowhere to be found. Kublai's rival had withdrawn, preserving what forces he could. Though his hold on the capital was lost, Ariq Boke was not yet ready to concede defeat. He

---

[i] Clements, Jonathan. *A Brief History of Khubilai Khan: Lord of Xanadu, Emperor of China.* 2010. Pg. 64.
[ii] Clements, Jonathan. *A Brief History of Khubilai Khan: Lord of Xanadu, Emperor of China.* 2010. Pg. 68.

regrouped elsewhere in the heartland and continued the fight, but with each passing month, his position grew weaker. Allies defected, supplies dwindled, and the empire's momentum shifted firmly in Kublai Khan's favor.

By 1264, with no path to victory remaining, Ariq Boke finally surrendered to his brother at Shangdu. Kublai Khan was not about to overlook the rebellion his brother had launched, though. Although Kublai Khan sought stability, he insisted on demonstrating that such defiance would not be ignored. After Ariq Boke's surrender, he was taken into custody and held under close supervision. There was no immediate execution or theatrical confrontation; instead, Kublai Khan allowed time to deliberate and consolidate his authority.

While Ariq Boke remained in confinement, Kublai Khan systematically removed many of his rival's key supporters from positions of influence. Although Kublai Khan might have desired peace, he was not willing to dismiss the civil war as a mere misunderstanding. His actions sent a clear message: the era of armed succession disputes was over.

Ariq Boke, once a powerful contender, now stood as a defeated and isolated figure. He lingered in a state of uncertain captivity, awaiting judgment. However, no formal trial ever came. In 1266, at around forty years old, Ariq Boke died. His death was officially recorded as unexplained, though some scholars suspect he was poisoned.

Whatever the case might have been, Kublai Khan was now firmly in control of the Mongol Empire. An assembly of notable Mongolians all hailed him as their supreme leader.

Demonstrating his newfound assertiveness, he decided to move the capital of the empire out of Karakorum and relocate it to the site of modern-day Beijing. This was a clear demonstration of the direction in which Kublai Khan wished to take the Mongol Empire. Whereas many of his predecessors wished to straddle the crossroads of Eurasia as they pushed farther into the Near East and eastern Europe, Kublai Khan was looking toward southern China. He desired to seize what remained of the once -great Song dynasty's possessions.

In time, Kublai Khan would indeed prove himself to be a worthy successor, and he would expand the Mongol Empire to an even greater extent than his grandfather Genghis Khan. But it was, of course, Genghis Khan who had started it all. He might have started out as an orphaned tribal nomad, but he eventually became the founder of a huge empire.

Chapter 9: Genghis Khan's Continued Impact on Modern-day Mongolians

"My descendants will dress themselves in clothes embroidered with gold; they will feed on exquisite dishes. They will ride superb coursers and hold the most beautiful young women in their arms. And they will have forgotten to whom they owe all that."

-Genghis Khan[1]

It is truly interesting to consider the fact that Mongolia today is a fairly obscure country and that much of its past—at least to the outside world—is not well known. Most people only know about Genghis Khan and the Mongol Empire. During the period of Genghis Khan's lifetime and a century or two afterward, Mongolian culture was able to project itself onto the world stage. Both before and after this period, Mongolia was more likely to be overshadowed by its powerful neighbors, namely Russia and China.

The fact that the Mongols during their high point had subdued and conquered Russia and China stands as an astonishing feat (and a continued source of embarrassment for both nations) in itself. As such, it is really no surprise that modern-day Mongolians might look back with a little bit of pride at Genghis Khan and his accomplishments.

---

[1] Hoang, Michel. *Genghis Khan.* 1988. Pg. 285.

Since some consider Genghis Khan to be nothing more than a bloodthirsty butcher, such reverence might be a bit offensive. But for Mongolians, Genghis Khan, for better or for worse, still represents the high point of Mongolian culture. If one were to travel to Mongolia, one could find Genghis Khan's image everywhere, from billboards to restaurant menus to even the currency. This is pretty interesting because no one is exactly sure what he even looked like! There are some vague sketches and several portraits made after his death, but no one really knows for sure. No one also really knows where the great khan was buried. In order to prevent anyone from desecrating his burial ground, his burial site has been kept secret for nearly one thousand years.

Genghis Khan on Mongolian currency. [12]

That push for secrecy began the moment that Genghis Khan died. This was initially done on the direct orders of Genghis Khan himself. As he lay dying in the spring of 1227, his armies were busy putting the final touches on the conquest of Western Xia. The great khan was so focused on the efforts of his troops that he ordered his failing health and even his possible death to be kept secret, lest his enemies learn of it.

He did not want his own death to serve as a rallying cry for his enemies. He did not want them to have a second wind and boost of confidence. The fact that Genghis Khan was so determined to secure victory, even if he did not personally live to see it, is a clear demonstration that he felt that the expansion of the Mongol Empire was bigger than himself. Many other leaders might have been focused on what they could do in their own lifetime and could have cared less about what might have happened after they were dead and gone. But not Genghis Khan. He clearly had the future in mind, and he wanted to ensure that the might of the Mongol Empire endured even after he had passed.

His forward-thinking nature is perhaps best exemplified by an old Mongolian account. While he lay dying, it is said that his family gathered around his deathbed. Each of them was given an arrow. They were not sure what they were to do with it or what the old khan intended by this gesture. But they soon found out. Genghis Khan told them to break the arrow. After they did so, he remarked on how easy it was to break that lone arrow and said that the same could be said of each and every one of them if they tried to go it alone. He then had each of them hold a large handful of arrows in one hand and ordered them to break the whole bundle at once. When they were unable to do so, Genghis Khan instructed them that if they stayed together as tightly as those bundles of arrows, no one would be able to break them.[i]

A 15th-century miniature of Genghis Khan on his deathbed handing the arrows to his sons.[13]

The Mongols were indeed an interesting bunch, and with Genghis Khan at the helm, they achieved heights of success that had not been seen before or even since. So, what are we to make of it all? Was there something unique about the Mongolians of this period, or was it all due to the uniqueness of that charismatic and ruthless leader known as

[i] Humphrey, Judy. *Genghis Khan: World Leaders Past & Present.* 1987. Pg. 105.

Genghis Khan? Can one person truly change history to such a degree by the sheer force of their own personality?

It is certainly stunning to consider such possibilities. There are a few other contenders for being personality game changers in history, such as Alexander the Great, Julius Caesar, and Napoleon Bonaparte, just to name a few. However, as it pertained to the success of Genghis Khan and his Mongolian horde, it was likely a combination of the khan's personality, as well as a multitude of other historical factors that occurred during this particular time and place, that allowed such things to happen.

There are likely young Mongolians today who are just as charismatic and innovative as young Temujin was, but due to certain conditions in the modern-day world, such as the hegemony of the three great powers—China, Russia, and the United States—they are left constrained to the steppes of their birth. Genghis Khan's rise coincided with a relatively dark age in Europe, and it happened during one of China's weakest historical periods.

As it pertained to China in particular, the Chinese were struggling to survive after an old thorn in their side, the Jurchen Jin, had pushed them to the southernmost reaches of the Chinese mainland. The ingenuity and brilliant strategies of Genghis Khan helped the Mongolians to defeat the Jurchen Jin, which put the Mongolians in a prime position to finish the job against China. Their momentum was so great and the khan's generals were so good that they were able to push in the opposite direction simultaneously, launching successful campaigns across central Asia, Iran, and the steppes of eastern Europe. This laid the groundwork for what would become the Ilkhanate, the Chagatai Khanate, and the Golden Horde. This was a remarkable feat, but without those aforementioned conditions, it likely would not have been possible.

One may not want to believe so much in fate or providence, but just the fact that he survived his childhood alone could be perceived as nothing short of a miracle. He was a fatherless child on the run, hunted and hounded by those who were much more powerful than he was. Yet through a combination of the kindness of strangers and his own grit and determination, he somehow managed to survive. He reached adulthood and gained a prominent position in the tribal hierarchy on the Mongolian steppes. Genghis Khan was then able to use his perch to consolidate his gains further and unite the tribes in larger and larger confederacies.

Genghis Khan conquered a vast swathe of land. As his time was nearing an end, he knew he did not have much longer for this world, so he began assigning successors to rule over various sections of his empire. This set up a pattern of various khanates or kingdoms, such as the Golden Horde in Russia and the Yuan dynasty in China. They were all ruled separately, although they were ostensibly all under the jurisdiction of one overlord, which would be the great universal khan.

A confluence of history and personality brought us this thought-provoking period in history. Even though some (certainly those who came out on the wrong end of it) might have viewed it as a dark and dire time, for those who enjoyed life under the Mongols, this was history at its very best.

His achievements have so far stood the test of time fairly well. The fact that he created the world's largest contiguous empire is still widely recognized to this very day. So, too, is the Mongol influence on the Silk Road and their ingenuity in warfare. The Mongols are credited with establishing a wide-reaching postal system that could effectively send messages from one end of the empire to the other.

The great Genghis Khan's descendants certainly have not forgotten his legacy. In fact, reverence for him still runs deep in Mongolia today. His name graces the nation's main airport, its central square, and even its currency. For modern-day Mongolians, he is more than a conqueror; he is the very founder of their identity as a people. And his family line continues on in staggering numbers. Genetic studies suggest that nearly half a percent of the world's male population—over sixteen million men—carry a Y-chromosome that can be traced back to Genghis Khan or one of his close male relatives. His bloodline, much like his empire once did, extends across much of Eurasia.

Conclusion: Genghis Khan's Greatest Legacy

Although religion was not a driving force for the Mongols, there were religious conflicts in many neighboring regions, such as the Middle East, Europe, and even, to some extent, East Asia. There were crusades and counter-crusades; it seemed as if there would be no end to people proclaiming that either the end was near or a new and glorious age was just about to dawn.

Genghis Khan boldly stepped into the midst of all of this. Initially, many of the religious partisans did not know quite what to make of him. Many were hopeful that he might be on their side—whatever side that might have been—and longed for him to aid them in their struggles.

The Christians hoped as much and even invented a long, rambling narrative about a great Christian ruler just to the east of the Muslim bloc, whom they dubbed Prester John. When Genghis Khan started smashing into the Islamic lands of the Khwarazmian Empire, many in the Christian West began to take notice and held out hope that maybe—just maybe—this Genghis Khan was living up to the legend of that Eastern Christian crusader.

Nevertheless, Genghis Khan often made use of religious musings for his own purposes. When he was laying waste to cities in the Khwarazmian Empire, he answered the puzzled cries of Muslim leaders who wondered aloud if they were being punished by God by publicly proclaiming to them that he was indeed the "scourge of God" who was sent to punish them. This was likely not what the tortured souls of his conquest wanted to hear, but it did line up with their worldview at the time. Many seemed to attribute every happenstance to whether or not they happened to be on God's side at that particular moment in time.

However, if the Christians thought that they were safe from the so-called "Scourge of God," they were mistaken. Once the Mongolian war machine started rolling through staunchly Christian lands such as Armenia, it seemed that all bets were off.

The Europeans discovered that Genghis Khan was not Prester John after all. He was (at least for the religious faithful of both Islam and Christianity) some other kind of strange and terrible force that had been unleashed. He seemed to be part of some sort of unstoppable whirlwind that had begun in the Mongolian steppes and reached just about all corners of the world (at least the known world at that time).

The Mongol Empire was already huge at the time of Genghis Khan's passing, but over the subsequent decades, his successors would make sure that it would grow even larger.

The fact that his empire continued to expand in such an astounding fashion even after his passing stands as a great testament to Genghis Khan's powerful and lasting legacy. He not only achieved greatness in his lifetime, but he also laid the groundwork for a stable foundation so that others could continue to build upon what he had begun.

After Genghis Khan died, the Mongol Empire certainly had its problems. The infighting between Kublai Khan and his brother Ariq Boke stands as a clear example of this. Nevertheless, the empire stayed together for the next few centuries after Genghis Khan's passing. It would later break apart into several feuding khanates, although complete disintegration would take some time.

The Mongol Empire deserves a high ranking on the list of the most powerful empires in history due to the fact that it held together for so long. This is perhaps Genghis Khan's greatest legacy. He was not just a world conqueror in his lifetime, but he was also the forger of a lasting and dynamic empire that seemed to know no natural bounds.

If you enjoyed this book, a review on Amazon would be greatly appreciated because it would mean a lot to hear from you.

To leave a review:

1. Open your camera app.
2. Point your mobile device at the QR code.
3. The review page will appear in your web browser.

Thanks for your support!

Here's another book by Enthralling History that you might like

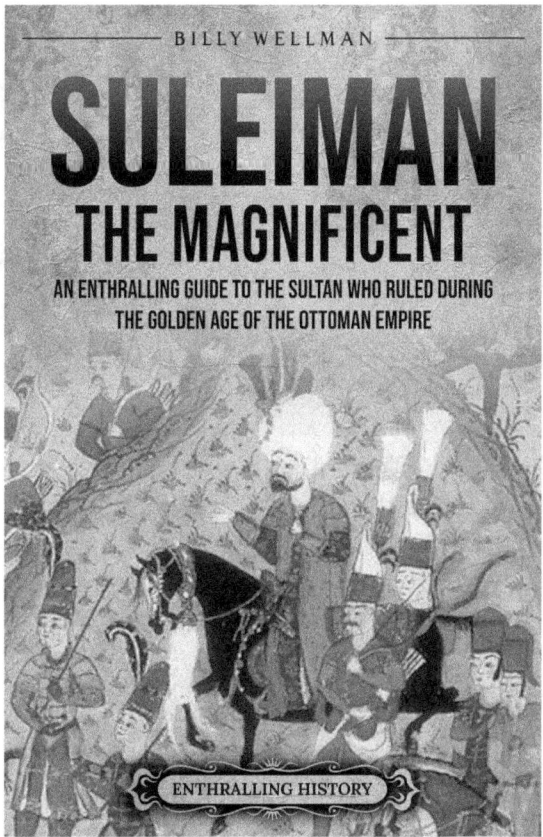

BILLY WELLMAN

SULEIMAN
THE MAGNIFICENT
AN ENTHRALLING GUIDE TO THE SULTAN WHO RULED DURING THE GOLDEN AGE OF THE OTTOMAN EMPIRE

ENTHRALLING HISTORY

Free limited time bonus

We forget 90% of everything
that we've read in 7 days...

Get the free printable pdf summary of
the book you've read AND much, much
more... shhhh...

Enter Your Most Frequently Used Email to Get Started

**DOWNLOAD FREE PDF
SUMMARY**

© Enthralling History

Stop for a moment. We have a free bonus set up for you. The problem is this: we forget 90% of everything that we read after 7 days. Crazy fact, right? Here's the solution: we've created a printable, 1-page pdf summary for this book that you're reading now. All you have to do to get your free pdf summary is to go to the following website: https://livetolearn.lpages.co/enthrallinghistory/

Or, Scan the QR code!

Once you do, it will be intuitive. Enjoy, and thank you!

Further Reading and Reference

Chambers, James. *Genghis Khan.* 2009.

Christian, David. *A History of Russia, Central Asia and Mongolia: Inner Eurasia from the Mongol Empire to Today, 1260-2000.* 1998.

Clements, Jonathan. *A Brief History of Khubilai Khan: Lord of Xanadu, Emperor of China.* 2010.

Colwell Miller, Connie. *History's Biggest Disasters: The Biggest Military Battles.* 2018.

Fitzhugh, William. *Genghis Khan and the Mongol Empire.* 2009.

Hoang, Michel. *Genghis Khan.* 1988.

Humphrey, Judy. *Genghis Khan: World Leaders Past & Present.* 1987.

Izzo, Robert. *The Life and Legend of Genghis Khan: Conquests, Power, Death, and the Mongol Empire.* 2020.

Nardo, Don. *Genghis Khan and the Mongol Empire.* 2010.

Plokhy, Serhii. *The Gates of Europe: A History of Ukraine.* 2015.

Sverdrup, Carl. *The Mongol Conquests: The Military Operations of Genghis Khan and Sube'etei.* 2017.

Image Sources

1   Chinneeb, CC BY-SA 3.0 <https://creativecommons.org/licenses/by-sa/3.0>, via Wikimedia Commons, https://commons.wikimedia.org/wiki/File:OnonRiver.jpg

2   JukoFF, CC BY-SA 4.0 <https://creativecommons.org/licenses/by-sa/4.0>, via Wikimedia Commons, https://commons.wikimedia.org/wiki/File:The_Hoelun_Monument_to_Genghis_Khan%27s_Mother_at_the_Mother_Hoelun_Memorial_Complex_in_Tsonjin_Boldog_02.jpg

3   Bernard Gagnon, CC0, via Wikimedia Commons, https://commons.wikimedia.org/wiki/File:Statue_at_Government_Palace,_Ulaanbaator_02.jpg

4   https://commons.wikimedia.org/wiki/File:Djengiz_Kh%C3%A2n_et_Toghril_Ong_Khan.jpeg

5   https://commons.wikimedia.org/wiki/File:YuanEmperorAlbumGenghisPortrait.jpg

6   Ganzorig Gavaa, CC BY-SA 2.0 <https://creativecommons.org/licenses/by-sa/2.0>, via Wikimedia Commons, https://commons.wikimedia.org/wiki/File:Burkhan_Khaldun_mount3.jpg

7   AirshipJungleman29, CC BY-SA 4.0 <https://creativecommons.org/licenses/by-sa/4.0>, via Wikimedia Commons, https://commons.wikimedia.org/wiki/File:Mongol_Empire_polities_circa_1200.png

8   https://commons.wikimedia.org/wiki/File:Tem%C3%BCjin_proclaimed_as_Genghis_Khan_in_1206_Jami%27_al-tawarikh_manuscript.jpg

9   https://commons.wikimedia.org/wiki/File:Jalal_al-Din_Khwarazm-Shah_crossing_the_rapid_Indus_river,_escaping_Chinggis_Khan_and_his_army.jpg

10 derivative work Bkkbrad / *File:Gengis Khan empire-fr.svg: historicair 17:01, 8 October 2007 (UTC), CC BY-SA 2.5 <https://creativecommons.org/licenses/by-

sa/2.5>, via Wikimedia Commons,
https://commons.wikimedia.org/wiki/File:Genghis_Khan_empire-switch.svg

11 https://commons.wikimedia.org/wiki/File:YuanEmperorAlbumOgedeiPortrait.jpg

12 Chinneeb, CC BY-SA 3.0 <https://creativecommons.org/licenses/by-sa/3.0>, via
Wikimedia Commons; https://commons.wikimedia.org/wiki/File:20000_Togrog.jpg

13 https://commons.wikimedia.org/wiki/File:Genghis_Khan_with_sons_
(Marco_Polo,_1400s).jpg